A SILVER PIECE OF CHANGE

Legacy Lessons Etched in the Cost of True Transformation

Ifedayo Greenway

& 7 Powerful Women Emerge from Their Cocoons, Handing Down Legacy and Valuable Coins of Transformation

Scripture quotations marked NLT are taken from the Holy Bible, New Living Translation Copyright © 1996, 2004, 2007, 2013, 2015 by Tyndale House Publishers Inc. Scripture quotations marked KJV are taken from the King James Version, Public domain. Scripture quotations marked MSG are taken from The Message Bible, Copyright © 1993, 1994, 1995, 1995, 1996, 2000, 2001, 2002 by Eugene H. Peterson. Scripture quotations are taken from The Holy Bible, New International Version® NIV® Copyright © 1973, 1978, 1984, 2011 by Biblica, Inc.™ Used by permission. All rights reserved worldwide

Printed in the United States of America

ISBN: 979-8-9994222-0-0

Ifedayo is available for speaking engagements, book signings, and workshops. Send your requests to ifegreenway@igandmore.com

Special discounts are available on bulk quantity purchases by book clubs, associations and special interests groups. For more details email: ifegreenway@igandmore.com

To the seekers of transformation,
Those who yearn to break free from the confines of the
cocoon,
And who are prepared to confront the true costs of their
journey toward change.

As you gather near the wise, eager to learn from the
generations that paved the way,
Embrace the priceless lessons encapsulated in their
experiences,
Ready to accept the valuable coins of knowledge crafted
through trials and reflection.

May you rise boldly into the vast unknown,
Confident that every tear, every challenge, and every
victory
Is refining you into the beautiful, resilient being you're
destined to become.

This message is for you—those courageous souls,
Who understand that profound change begins from within,
And that wisdom resides in recognizing the journey as both
an honor and a duty.
Let the narratives of the wise illuminate your path,
As you gracefully embark on your transformative flight.

Contents

Foreword

Darlene Northam

I hated her! Yeah, I know it sounds hard-hearted to say that about your mother, but I did. She didn't see the value in me or that of my sisters. As a broken woman, it appeared to be all about what she wanted. Maybe it was her low self-esteem or the fact she was married to a whore, my dad, which prevented her from being a nurturer. As a young girl, I could only process at my level of understanding. So, in my opinion, my sisters and I would always come second; we had to figure it out. Unfortunately, when my dad abandoned us, she repeated the cycle of making her boyfriends the priority. In my moments of reflection, I found myself asking God why I couldn't have a mom who showed love and affection to her daughters. When I didn't receive an answer, I became angry and shouted at the top of my lungs to Him, "Thanks for the crappy life you dealt me!"

In my mind's eye, being the eldest of nine meant the deck was stacked against me. Although I wasn't adopted, I often fantasized that there had to be another set of parents out there—my real parents—who would one day find me and rescue me from it all. It was a comforting illusion, a way to escape the painful truth that the dysfunction I experienced growing up didn't begin with me. It was generational, and I be damned if I would walk in my mom's footsteps. As I got older, I vowed never to follow in her footsteps—bearing child after child for a man who didn't love me. I also promised myself I would never neglect to create time and space for the children I brought into the world. Still, I couldn't escape the reality that I shared her DNA—a constant reminder that, like it or not, she was my mother.

Needless to say, I was battling demons I hadn't created. As a result, I was hell-bent on not becoming her. But ironically, in so many ways, I was her—choosing the wrong men, having children outside of marriage, and struggling with the same low self-esteem I so deeply resented in her. What a hypocrite I was. I lacked the maturity to raise the two beautiful daughters I birthed, and ultimately, I gave my oldest to her father to raise. To escape my regret and feelings of damnation, I turned to alcohol, indulging in it regularly, and engaged in reckless living. It wasn't until I got tired of my own shit that I decided to change the narrative of my story. I started back attending church, and it was there that I met my amazing husband. We had a child together and began a life that, although not perfect, was full of promise. He taught me how to love, and how to be the wife and mother he and our children needed. What an oxymoron! The very things I should've learned from a mother—how to nurture, how to be emotionally present, how to care for a family—were instead taught to me by a man, at a time when all I knew from men was abandonment and broken trust. Although I never had those roles modeled for me growing up, he became my example of what love and nurturing truly looked like.

Because of his care and attention to detail, I began to walk in a level of faith, sensitivity, encouragement, and patience that I had not experienced before. So much so, that God uprooted my husband to Charlotte, NC where we served as head ministry leaders for three-and-a-half years. Surrounded by a diversity of women from all walks of life, I embraced the opportunity to step out of my comfort zone and love them with an authentic heart, sharing my life's story. As a result, the shame I once held as a curse no longer plagued me. My transparency drew women of all ages and backgrounds to me as a woman of wisdom. Over the years of evolving, God placed three amazing young women in my life whom I eventually adopted as my own. Me, really! God got jokes! After our assignment in Charlotte, we returned to Virginia where I became the lead for the Women's Ministry (The Titus Touch) at my church, which was founded on the principles of Titus 2:3-5. Knowing that I could not lead these women solo, I sought out Ifedayo Greenway to assist me, and she graciously accepted. Alongside Ifedayo and I were six other women who made up the core group. Among those courageous divas was my daughter, the one I once gave to her father to raise. Isn't it paradoxical how God can use our pain to create something beautiful and meaningful? Talk about transformation! I believe that my ability to see past my own mishaps gave me the motivation to be a lifeline for someone else. As a ministry, our intentionality and commitment to see women healed and whole, impacted the lives of those who sat at our feet.

Oddly enough, When Ifedayo approached me to write the foreword for her remarkable work, I was initially uncertain if I was the right person for the task. As a result, I requested some time to pray about it. During this reflection, I was reminded of the many women I have counseled and mentored over the years. Until that moment, I had not fully realized the countless nights I spent praying for young women struggling with anxiety and depression. On numerous occasions, I dedicated my time and resources to ensure that the women I helped left my presence feeling better than when they arrived. All of the experiences I encountered on my journey, I now wear as badges of honor. In all of that, I would say, she asked the right person. I am another seasoned woman willing to spare some vital nuggets with anyone who is willing to put in the work on the front end because it will all pay off in the end.

Well, as a world-renowned visionary author, writing coach for women, teacher, motivational speaker, entrepreneur, and mother, Ifedayo has done it again. This book, "A Silver Piece of Change, is more than a collection of stories shared by a few seasoned women sixty and older as a means of assisting other women in navigating life's twists and turns.

Thus, it offers insights into how to endure the hard times, celebrate the good ones, and find meaning in the moments in between. For every woman who has ever wondered if she has the strength to keep going, these pages serve as a reminder that you are not alone. As you turn these pages, may you find inspiration, courage, and solidarity. May the wisdom of these veteran women remind you that even in life's messiest moments there is splendor. May their stories encourage you to embrace your journey with an open heart, knowing that each step, no matter how small, is a testament to your resilience.

"Older women are to teach the young women to love their husbands and children. They are to teach them to think before they act, to be pure, to be workers at home, to be kind, and to obey their own husbands. In this way, the Word of God is honored."

— Titus 2: 4-5 (NLV)

Sitting Indian Style at the Feet of Wisdom

Ifedayo Greenway

Silence infiltrated the room and we all stared in awe as she made her way to the platform. Every step was a testament to her strength as she was visibly struggling with physical ailments. I had known her since I was a little girl growing up in my Dad's church and affectionately called her Ma-Marian. I was astonished as I watched her make her way across the pulpit because, before that day, it had been well over 20 years since I had seen her. I grew up knowing her as one of the "church mamas"; not because of her age, but because all the kids loved and flocked to her like she was their mama. She directed the youth choir and she had this way of drawing the younger generation to her nurturing heart. But that day, after not seeing her for so long, it was clear that she had not only aged but that life had taken a toll on her health and physical body. Positioning herself to complete her assignment, her feet slid across the platform with the help of her walking cane and she sat her sick body in the chair that had been strategically placed for her. Despite the challenges of older age and physical limitations, Ma-Marian showed up with an unwavering purpose as the keynote speaker at a women's conference I was attending. Ironically, the theme of the conference was Renewal [to make like new, restore to freshness, vigor, or perfection]. Though her body moved slower, her words flowed freely; gentle yet potent, settling on our hearts like much-needed water on dry and thirsty plants. Seated at the front of the room, she became a wellspring of wisdom. With grace and grit, she poured herself into a room full of women hungry for healing and truth. The moment felt so surreal and almost cinematic. I was sitting next to one of my "sista-friends" who also grew up in the same church I did with Ma-Marian. After about five minutes of listening to her speak, she leaned in and whispered, "I would love to sit Indian style at her feet."

I couldn't have concurred any quicker. It was a longing to be close and in a vulnerable position to receive the wisdom you don't often find anymore. The kind of insight that couldn't be taught in classrooms but was only earned through a lifetime of walking with God. Her words were layered with a depth only the seasoned soul possesses. Ma-Marian chose to share and expound on the story of Mephibosheth (a name that ties our tongues for sure - so don't ask me how to pronounce it) from 2 Samuel in the Bible. She told his story with such compassion that it didn't feel ancient or distant; it felt like ours. I listened with intensity, it felt as if she were narrating my own life story up to that point, and I was desperate to learn how to be renewed and restored from the weight of that narrative. You see when he was a baby, Mephibosheth's nurse picked him up and subsequently dropped him from her arms while she was trying to escape from their enemies. The accident left him physically paralyzed and emotionally diminished. He grew up internalizing that fall, defining himself by what had happened to him; being dropped by someone who was supposed to be his caregiver. At one point in the story, he even referred to himself as a "dead dog", a metaphoric description that seems to be a vivid reflection of his shattered identity and wounded self-worth. As Ma-Marian spoke, her words stirred something in us and unlocked a collective memory. It was clear by the emotions in the room and the tears falling from many of our faces that we were mentally revisiting the moments we had been "dropped" by people we trusted, loved, or depended on. I started to think about and remember instances where people were put in place to shield or nurture me, but instead, they became the very source of some of my deepest pain. I recalled the sting of being intentionally mishandled. The kind of calculated betrayal that cripples not just the body, but the soul. When I was studying to become a minister, the church assigned me to a mentor, an older woman who was supposed to train me. She had the opportunity to use both her life experiences and academic training to pour into me, to teach me critical lessons about what it meant to operate in the calling of a preacher. One day, she challenged me to prepare a sermon and deliver it to my peers, who were also in training for ministry. With fear tingling in my feet, I rose to the challenge and stepped to the podium. When I finished, my peers were clapping, cheering, encouraging me, and clearly moved by what I had shared. But she...she looked me dead in my face, with the residue of her unresolved bitterness in her eyes, and said, "The people will never receive you. They will never listen to anything you have to say." She dropped me. She broke my "speaking/preaching spirit" in places I didn't even know could be broken; especially since I was just a novice. That moment crippled my pulpit self-esteem for many years to come. Every time I stood to speak after that, I wrestled with the paralyzing thought that no one would accept what I had to say. I couldn't understand why she didn't choose to use her influence differently in my life. Even if I had completely missed the mark on that sermon, she had an opportunity—a silver one—to create a teachable moment, to leave a legacy lesson in the life of a younger woman who was genuinely counting on her wisdom. But instead, she chose to weaponize criticism, using it as a tool to crush rather than cultivate. She managed the moment not with grace, but with a personal vendetta, one I later discovered stemmed from a lingering misunderstanding between us. I spent a lot of time in therapy digging up the rejection seed she planted, a seed sown not in ignorance but with intention. She didn't just drop me, she made a deliberate decision to throw me to the floor, serving vengeance instead of guidance.

Sadly, that wasn't the only time I experienced the pain of being let go by someone I looked up to. Later in life, I connected with another woman—a well-respected figure in the church and a known force for pushing empowerment in the community. I vividly remember the day she called to tell me she believed God had told her she was meant to cover me in my speaking and writing my ministry. She spoke with conviction, saying she felt assigned to my life as a designated leader—someone who would offer prayer, spiritual protection, guidance, and accountability.

After accepting her into my life, she began referring to me as her spiritual daughter. It felt like a Naomi-and-Ruth connection—one drawn from the Bible, where Ruth's unwavering loyalty to Naomi and Naomi's wise guidance helped shape a new path for Ruth's life. Their bond was one of love, faith, and mutual support. That's what I hoped we would embody.

At first, I believed her intentions were pure—and maybe they were. But over time, it became apparent that what may have started as sincere guidance was being diluted by ego, entitlement, and a controlling nature. Speaking up for myself eventually became the dividing line. One disagreement unraveled everything she had once claimed to be in my life. What hurt the most wasn't just the fallout—it was discovering that she had shared a skewed version of our disagreement with others, in ways that damaged my reputation and my business.

I was deeply hurt—not only because I held her in such high esteem, but because I truly depended on her to help me grow. From the outside, the public accolades suggested she was pouring into and uplifting others—and in many ways, she was. But behind the scenes, there were moments that left me feeling dismissed and wounded. That's not how I imagined a spiritual mother would treat her spiritual daughter.

As a woman of much wisdom and a mother figure, she had the opportunity to choose restoration over rejection. Had she chosen to lean into grace, we both might have learned meaningful lessons about forgiveness and what it means to love beyond conflict. I had hoped for that kind of unconditional love, but what I received in the end felt more like abandonment—followed by whispers in the community and silence whenever we crossed paths again.

Let me be clear: this isn't about character bashing, and I'm not here to paint either of these women as villains. I've had moments in my own life when I didn't get the assignment right either, and I take full responsibility for my part in the misunderstandings and fallouts. But I also believe there's a weighty responsibility that comes with stepping into a leadership or mentoring role—especially when you declare yourself a spiritual covering. When you're entrusted to lead, how you navigate conflict, extend grace, and model maturity can leave a lasting imprint. So I don't see myself as a victim in these stories—they're real experiences that shaped me. Times when I felt betrayed by women I believed had been sent to teach and uplift. They were painful, and they were hard to forgive. But in time, they taught me to deeply value the authentic wisdom voices in my life—those who correct with compassion and walk with integrity.

Thankfully, that day while Ma-Marian was speaking she didn't just name the pain; she pointed us to the power of restoration. She highlighted that even when we've been mishandled, misjudged, or mistreated, healing is still possible. We may not be able to rewrite what others have done, but we can reclaim what remains. We can gather the pieces, rise from the low places, and step into legacy. That's what Ma-Marian did when she offered her life, her voice, and her wisdom as a generational gift. That moment of listening to Ma-Marian will forever be etched in my core memories as something sacred. I think it was the refreshing feeling of truly being present, the quiet joy of slipping into the purest childlike moment and using my imagination to see myself postured at her feet as she taught us invaluable lessons on healing and becoming new.

Imagine a child sitting cross-legged at the feet of a wise grandmother or a seasoned elder. Picture a student on a colorful rug during storytime, listening to their teacher read a story. The teacher shares illustrations and uses different voices for each character, transforming a simple story into a heartwarming adventure. In school, we referred to this sitting position as "crisscross applesauce," but it is also known as sitting "Indian style." It's one of the most natural ways to feel grounded. That position, for many children, signaled it was time to pause, focus, and lean in. But perhaps, that sitting stance is not just for children. And maybe, just maybe for adults, it's not about the physical posture at all. It's a soul posture of stillness, humility, and intentional listening, not with our bodies, but with our hearts and minds unguarded, wide opened, and surrendered. Now, I promise I'm not about to turn this chapter into a full-blown Bible study but go with me for a second. There's a story in Luke 10 that captures this perfectly. Jesus stops by the home of two sisters—Martha and Mary. Martha, being the hospitable one, is in go mode: cleaning, prepping, and making sure everything is just right. Mary sees an opportunity and takes it. She positions herself at Jesus' feet and engages in His teaching, soaking up every word He speaks because she recognizes the value of His presence. Martha, understandably frustrated, calls her sister out: "For real Jesus, I know you lyin'! I'm doing all the work while she just sits there in your face?" And Jesus, in His gentle way, redirects her, not by scolding her for being angry, but by shifting her perspective. He says, "Martha, you're doing a lot, but only one thing truly matters right now—and Mary chose it." Mary had chosen to sit Indian style at the feet of wisdom. Now, here's the real version of those scriptures, cause' surely you know I finessed that conversation in my tone and imagination right...Lol?

Luke 10: 38-42 (NLT Version)

38 As Jesus and the disciples continued on their way to Jerusalem, they came to a certain village where a woman named Martha welcomed him into her home. 39 Her sister, Mary, sat at the Lord's feet, listening to what he taught. 40 But Martha was distracted by the big dinner she was preparing. She came to Jesus and said, "Lord, doesn't it seem unfair to you that my sister just sits here while I do all the work? Tell her to come and help me."

41 But the Lord said to her, "My dear Martha, you are worried and upset over all these details! 42 There is only one thing worth being concerned about. Mary has discovered it, and it will not be taken away from her.

What helped me see the biblical narrative in a more aligned way with what I'm sharing in this chapter was the fact that the story could've simply said Mary was *listening* to Jesus. But it didn't. It made a point to tell us she was *sitting at His feet.* Why? Because posture matters. That detail gave us a deeper, more in-depth, and layered insight into the moment. She didn't just tune her ears to Jesus' teaching, she was present in a soul-snatching kind of way (and yes, you do know Jesus is the one and true soul-snatcher). She was all in, no matter what was happening around her or what others thought of her decision to sit. She humbled herself, made emotional room to receive, and positioned her heart to learn from the greatest of all time (the bonafide G.O.A.T).

And that... ***that part,*** is what this chapter is really about.

There are seasons in our lives when we're up and running, building, pushing, managing, fixing, hosting, and creating. But then there are vital life-pivoting moments when we're invited to sit. To stop striving. To let go of control. Acknowledging that we don't have all the answers, which allows us to be open to learning from others. It's an invitation to RSVP (respond if you please) to the open seat in the classroom of wisdom and humility. When we embrace humility, we give ourselves the freedom to seek knowledge without the pressure of knowing everything. And that stance of surrender is where you receive the invaluable coins of true transformation. So today, the invitation isn't to do more—but to sit a little lower, a little quieter. Maybe it's time to cross your legs, ground your spirit, and lean into the presence of something greater than yourself. Because sometimes, wisdom doesn't chase us down, it waits for us to sit still enough to notice it.

I'm sure Ma-Marian never imagined that long after her passing, I'd be writing about the impact she had on my adult life through that one encounter. And honestly, if it hadn't been for that day, the memories of what it was like growing up with her in church might have quietly faded into the background. But that moment brought it all back and left a lasting imprint. That!...is the power of legacy moving forward. Her words became more than a moment, they became a message to me that I can now pass on to you. What she deposited in me that day didn't stay rooted in the past; it grew with me, spoke to me in new seasons, and ultimately shaped the way I show up in the world. Wisdom is what you carry within—the ability to apply knowledge, experience, and insight with discernment, compassion, and depth. It is often cultivated through life's trials, personal reflection, and intentional growth. Legacy, on the other hand, is what you leave behind—your lasting impact, influence, or contribution that continues after you're gone. While legacy can include tangible accomplishments, it's often the intangible things, the decisions you make, the values you live by, and the insight you pass down that hold the most weight. The beauty of legacy and wisdom being intertwined is that legacy is not just about what is left behind it's about having the wisdom to know how to use it to live on. I've been blessed to sit at the feet of many wise women and experience the inheritance of their wisdom. Ma-Marian is one of them, but she's certainly not the only one. Each of these women has shared sacred moments with me. Their words, their presence, and their posture continue to shape the woman I'm becoming.

My mother sang a little song to me for years:

"I wish I had a little red box to put Dayo in,

I'd kiss and kiss and kiss and kiss,

And put her right back in."

That song became a consistent rhythm in my life. And ironically, it taught me to live beyond the box, to embrace life fully and fearlessly.

My Godmother, Mama Gwen, reminds me time and time again of God's unconditional love. Her simple texts— *"Your Daddy loves you"* always come right when I need them most. In seasons when I doubted God's nearness, those words anchored me. They quite literally saved my spiritual life. She taught me the value of opening yourself up to love that doesn't have to come from genetic ties—love that finds you anyway.

My best friend, Sandra, in the most unflamboyant ways, showed me that my authentic voice is a superpower. Not by preaching it, but by creating a safe space where I could simply be—unfiltered, unpolished, and still fully embraced. Her quiet consistency, her unwavering belief in me, and the way she listens without trying to fix me have all modeled what true friendship looks like. Without even knowing it, she helped to heal and gently piece back together the brokenness left behind by past friendships that mishandled my heart. She's never demanded the spotlight. Through her, I learned that true friends don't just walk beside you; they help restore the parts of you that have forgotten what trust feels like.

And then there's my sister-friend and editor, Monique. She left her mark on my heart during the editing of my memoir with just one sentence: "*Even babies are born during a storm.*" That line stopped me in my tracks. It reminded me that purpose doesn't wait for perfection. It pushes through pain, through chaos, through uncertainty. Her words breathed courage into me on days when doubt was loud and the journey felt too heavy. At that moment, she wasn't just editing my manuscript, she was editing my mindset. And I'll never forget it.

Those are just a few of the women who have poured into me, who have helped shape both the wisdom I carry and the legacy I'm building; one that I hope to leave for my daughters and granddaughters. I asked my daughter Miya and my goddaughter Nevaeh (or Lil Girl, as I affectionately call her) this: *What is one legacy lesson you hope I leave with you as your mother or godmother?*

Miya was seeking a legacy lesson around the power of her words and how they can shape the world around her. She said,

"Learn that no matter the situation, your words and tone can really dictate everything. They can shape how people feel and respond. And sometimes, even if you didn't mean to hurt someone, it's important to give them space to heal how they need to."

Nevaeh's heart was set on me passing down wisdom gained on motherhood, She said,

"How to be a good mom and keep a relationship with God."

While coaching and conversing with one of the writers featured in this book, I asked her a simple yet profound question: *"What would you say to my daughter if she came to you with questions about life?"* I encouraged her to write from a perspective of passing down a valuable experience, not only to my daughter but to every young woman who comes after her.

In the chapters ahead, you'll hear from women who have done exactly that. Each one of them is 60 years or older—seasoned by time, graced by God, shaped by experience, and deeply rooted in wisdom. They've lived through storms and still carry strength. And because of that, they are more than qualified to hand down *a silver piece of change*—legacy lessons and life coins that you and the next generation can use to cover the cost of true transformation.

These women accepted the assignment of sharing their lives; not just the pretty polished parts, but the real, raw, and redemptive parts too. Their stories are personal and powerful. Their insights are earned. They are giving from the deepest wells of their lived experience, pouring out truth, and timeless intellect from the vaults of their hearts.

So I invite you: to sit, breathe, reflect, and receive.

You are about to sit at the feet of wisdom.

Live the Lesson

Reflection Page

Imagine sitting at the feet of Ifedayo, soaking in the wisdom she just shared in this chapter. Let her story speak to your heart as you reflect on how it connects to your own journey.

1. The Lesson that Resonates?

What moment or message in this chapter resonated with you most?

Why do you think it stood out? (Write your response below)

_____

_____

_____

2. Imagining a Conversation

With her wisdom still fresh in your mind, what's one question you would ask Ifedayo for further insight or clarity. Feel free to email her—her contact information is at the end of this book. *(Write your question below)*

_____

_____

_____

3. Reflection in Action

Sometimes, reflection needs to move beyond words. What is one action you can take today to honor the message in this chapter? *(Describe your action below)*

_____

_____

_____

Your Thoughts:

This is more than reflection — it's transformation in motion. Let this chapter's wisdom shape the legacy you're creating, one decision, one act, one change at a time. *(Use this space to write freely. Let your heart respond, not just your mind.)*

_____

_____

_____

Life Interrupted, Legacy Intact

Gwendolyn Winston-Marrow

I am a writer. I began crafting my chapter for the collaboration *"A Silver Piece of Change"* with purpose and passion. But then—life interrupted. No… life shattered the script I had written for myself. In February, my husband passed away. Living without him in the middle of this creative journey was never part of my outline. I won't go into the details here—but know this: life and grief rewrote everything.

Jeremiah 29:11 reminds me: *"For I know the plans I have for you," declares the Lord, "plans to prosper you and not to harm you, plans to give you hope and a future."*

God knew my husband's passing would become part of my story, long before I ever could have imagined it. He also knew my voice still mattered. That there were still words in me, even if the story I'm telling now looks nothing like the one I planned.

This isn't the chapter I expected, but these are the words that He's called me to write. Allow me to share my *Silver Piece of Change:*

- **Don't settle.** Don't stay in a place where you're not truly being loved—just to meet someone else's expectations or to keep up appearances. You deserve a love that's real, mutual, and whole. Not one that only looks good on the outside but leaves you empty on the inside.

- **Be authentic in your relationships.** You never know when a relationship will change or come to an end, and you may not always get another chance to say what's real, to be fully seen and fully honest. Even if the other person isn't ready to talk, say what you need to say.

- **Free yourself with the truth.** Because healing often begins with what you're brave enough to express.

- Let me encourage you: when you have the opportunity to speak your truth, speak it. Even when it's hard. Even when it hurts. Share it anyway. There is healing in honesty. There is freedom in release.

Speak what's on your heart.

Don't hold it in.

Don't wait for a "better" time or tell yourself, *"I'll do it tomorrow."*

When the Spirit of God prompts you—that is the time.

Trust that leading. That moment is sacred.

Though these words were originally shared with my beautiful *Silver* collaborators, I believe God has something to say to you, too. Whether you're writing a book or being called to a completely different assignment, the message remains the same: **Lean in. Listen closely.**

God has a way of drawing out the gift within you, but it starts with surrender.

When you open yourself up to Him and say, *"Yes, Lord, use me,"* that's when He moves. But when you say, *"I can't,"* and stay stuck in fear or doubt, He waits—because He's ready, but He's also waiting on your willingness.

That's exactly what He's done through this book.

That's what He's done in each of you.

Even when you wanted to say *no*, even in the middle of your process—those moments when you were writing and thinking, *"Lord, can I really say this? What will people think?"*—God kept saying, write it anyway.

And guess what? He wouldn't let you take it out. Because obedience matters more than approval.

Legacy Lesson:

There comes a point in your journey where you stop editing your truth to make others comfortable. You learn to obey

God and trust Him with the outcome. If you're constantly worried about what people will think, you'll never be authentic, and your voice will lose its power.

So don't overthink it. Don't water it down. Don't reshape your message to please others.

Write it how God gave it to you.

Say it exactly the way He placed it in your spirit.

And when you do, you'll stand back and be amazed—not just at what you wrote, but at what God did through your obedience.

You'll be proud.

He'll be proud.

And you will be in awe of the fruit that comes from you being obedient to God.

Live the Lesson

Reflection Page

Imagine sitting at the feet of Gwendolyn, soaking in the wisdom she just shared in this chapter. Let her story speak to your heart as you reflect on how it connects to your own journey.

1. The Lesson that Resonates?

What moment or message in this chapter resonated with you most?

Why do you think it stood out? (Write your response below)

_____

_____

_____

2. Imagining a Conversation

With her wisdom still fresh in your mind, what's one question you would ask Gwendolyn for further insight or clarity. Feel free to email her—her contact information is at the end of this book. *(Write your question below)*

_____

_____

_____

3. Reflection in Action

Sometimes, reflection needs to move beyond words. What is one action you can take today to honor the message in this chapter? *(Describe your action below)*

_____

_____

_____

Your Thoughts:

This is more than reflection—it's transformation in motion. Let this chapter's wisdom shape the legacy you're creating, one decision, one act, one change at a time. *(Use this space to write freely. Let your heart respond, not just your mind.)*

_____

_____

_____

Silenced By His Sexuality

Joyce Freeman

The day my father kicked my older brother out of the house for coming out as gay was the day I muted my voice at home and stopped asking my parents questions. That day, I lost my voice. I grew up in a household with three siblings – two brothers and a sister. My family was deeply involved in a Baptist church, where my father served as a deacon and my mother sang in the choir. Being curious at a young age, my questions were "Why this?" and "Why that?" The responses were always "Do as I say" or "That's grown folks' business."

I loved all of my siblings, but was especially close to my oldest brother, who was eight years older than me. I looked up to him for his strength, leadership, and intelligence. He encouraged me to always be the best version of myself, no matter what others said. The day he made the decision to tell my parents that he was gay, changed our lives forever. He was graduating from college soon and had accepted a position in another state. I think that he decided to tell the family because he was hoping that our parents would accept him. I believe that my mom always knew, but never said anything because she knew my father would never accept that he had a gay son. I was around 10 or 11 years old and my brother and sister were too young to understand. To me, it didn't matter; he was still my brother.

This news hit my dad hard. He was hurt, embarrassed, and angry. No one talked openly about family members or friends being gay, also known as "in the closet." It was never discussed in our church. My mom tried to calm my dad to talk about it, but he refused. From the day that my brother was kicked out, he was never discussed in our house again. I wanted to ask questions, but I was afraid that the same thing would happen to me.

After my brother was put out of the house, my parents' relationship was never the same. I was 13 years old when my mom and dad separated. There may have been other things going on, but they never sat down with us to talk about the separation. I came home from school one day only to find out that my mom was no longer there. I asked my dad what happened. He only said that they could not live with each other anymore, so he told her to leave the house, but we had to stay with him. Remember, I lived in a time when grown folks' business was never discussed with children. To this day, I have questions that I haven't received answers to, but God and therapy has helped me understand that my parents did only what they knew to do. I shouldn't judge them, but instead give them honor and grace.

As the oldest, I became responsible for taking care of my siblings, keeping the house clean, cooking, etc. I didn't ask why and just did what I was supposed to. I found out from my brother that my mom had moved with him in Philadelphia, PA. He settled there after graduating from college. She was getting herself together to find a job and a home so that my brother, sister and I could eventually move with her. My brother knew that I had taken on adult responsibilities and was the caregiver of my family. He knew what I was going through, but couldn't do anything about the situation because he was not welcomed in our home. We didn't know how to help each other. We both had been silenced.

Eventually, my mom got a home and my siblings and I had to decide if we wanted to move in with her. So much time had passed and I was 17, getting ready to graduate from high school. Afterwards, I planned to take a year off from school to travel to Paris, France, and then return to attend Norfolk State University in Virginia. I didn't want to start college until I knew what I wanted to major in. I chose Paris because of the culture, clothes, food, and most important, the Eiffel Tower. I didn't know anyone in Paris so, to some, it may have seemed like a crazy idea. I was a young girl who had never been anywhere outside of her neighborhood, but I saw the trip as my freedom—a way to regain my voice. My favorite aunt (my dad's sister), told me that when I graduated from college, she would pay for my trip, an apartment, and provide funds for me while I was there. My aunt and uncle had the resources to take care of my expenses. They had their own businesses—a small confectionary store and built homes for sale on land that they owned. She never explained why she would do this for me, but I believe that it was because I didn't have a chance to enjoy my childhood. Just when I thought that my life was getting better, I found out that I was pregnant.

I met my child's father at a friend's house party. He did not attend the same school as me, but we continued to talk, and eventually date. We dated for a year before I became pregnant. Back then, when a young girl got pregnant, she was either sent away to live with a relative until she had the child or she got married. This forced marriage was called a "shotgun wedding". So, I married the father of my daughter and attempted to do everything to make the marriage work, like pleasing him and not asking questions.

We both were young and had no clue what we were doing. A year later, our marriage became physical and verbally abusive. I justified staying after the abuse began because I felt that I didn't do enough to please him, so it was my fault. When my brother found out, he helped me get back on my feet and encouraged me to not let the past define me. I was also supported by my village—a group of sister friends, who I confided in. They each took turns letting me and my daughter stay in their homes. The plan was to move from house to house until I could get on my feet. I didn't want to stay in one place too long, fearing that my husband could do something to harm them or someone in their family.

I recall one day he found me off the school campus I attended and attempted to force me to come back. I truly believe that God gave me the strength to use my voice that day, though I was scared to say that I wasn't going with him. I don't know if it was the look in my eyes or the tone of my voice, but he said "You're crazy," and walked away. I said to God, "Was that all I had to do?" With this chapter of my life closed, I was able to refocus, take care of my child, find a job, and return to college.

I graduated in May 1989 with a degree in Public Administration. I wanted to become a case manager, working for Social Services, however, I accepted a position as a Human Resources Specialist with the federal government. I recruited and placed new employees into government positions. I served in that role and another position as an Equal Employment Opportunity (EEO) Specialist, where I provided guidance to managers and resolved complaints filed by employees who believed that they had been discriminated against through mediation. I retired from the federal government after 28 years in October 2013. During my career, I felt that I was regaining my voice and I was being heard. Until my brother's death.

Losing my brother when I was 28 years old was the most painful experience of my life. That day, I came home from work and received a phone call from one of his friends. He told me that my brother had been found in his apartment stabbed to death, I fell to my knees, and totally lost it. I felt like I had been stabbed in my stomach. I lost a part of myself because of our strong bond. I lost my best friend, my confidant, my encourager, my voice. I was in a daze from the time I was told, throughout the service, and at the gravesite. Talking to family members was worthless because they still had not accepted the fact that he was gay.

My mother was in shock, too. She grieved deeply from the day my brother died in 1980 until her own passing in 2004. After his death, she withdrew from her friends and stopped socializing altogether, only leaving the house for grocery runs and doctor appointments. She passed after being diagnosed with Alzheimer's disease. I believe that my dad grieved because he had lost his son and felt guilty for kicking him out of our home. He never talked about it and carried his thoughts and feelings to his grave in 2002.

I didn't know how to cope with my brother's death. My grief was so deep that I felt guilty and wished that I had a chance to see and talk to him before he died. *Did he know who took his life? Did my brother suffer before he took his last breath?* I didn't know anything about going to a therapist or talking to a Pastor, since I wasn't going to church much before his death. I had no one to talk to about my grief, so I kept all of my emotions locked inside. I knew how my family felt about my brother's lifestyle, so I dared not talk to them about my grief because they didn't know what to say. I attempted to have conversations about our deceased parents and brother with my siblings, but they were dealing with their grief differently, maybe because they were younger. My daughter was too young to understand the relationship dynamics that I had with my family and my brother's lifestyle. Every time I felt that I had conquered finding my voice, I would go back into my protection shell for fear of who I would hurt or how people would react.

I went through relationship after relationship, even getting married a second time—not for love, but out of loneliness. I was involved with men who had their own trauma so we had no real connection. I was dealing with their trauma as well as mine and was afraid to express my emotions, physically or verbally, in any of my relationships. My actions consisted of catering to their every need and not considering my own for fear of abuse. I lost my voice and my identity, doing any and everything to make them happy so that they wouldn't leave me.

In my professional relationships, I remained silent. I struggled to use my voice at work because I didn't want confrontation and was fearful there would be hostility toward me if I made suggestions. I became the "behind the scenes person," making sure that everything was going well, though I felt things could have been done another way. I called it "people pleasing." I was seen but not heard, which goes back to not asking questions as a child. I put on a "happy face," even though I was still missing my brother, still grieving.

In the year 2020—40 years after my brother's death—came a revelation for me to start understanding everything that I had gone through in my life. During the COVID lockdown, I started a journal going back as far as I could remember about my childhood to help me understand how my parents raised us. I wanted to get answers so that I could heal. I wanted to regain my voice because I had a lot to say and didn't want to continue sitting in that pit of grief and pain. I decided to find a therapist that would help me on my journey. I found someone but was placed on a waitlist due to COVID. In the meantime, I restarted journaling so that I would not fall back into a rut again. I started connecting with God more than I ever did in the past. God has always been a part of my life, however, I had put Him in the background, choosing to please everyone but Him. During the pandemic, there were no distractions, so I could stay in His Word, which became an important part of my healing process.

In 2022, a "God-wink" moment (an answered prayer) took place during a Women's Health Conference that I attended. There were five women on the panel discussing ways to take care of oneself spiritually, physically, emotionally, and mentally. When the therapist on the panel introduced herself I realized that she was the same person I spoke to in 2020. When I shared with her that I was on her waitlist, she looked at her calendar and set up an appointment for me the next week.

When we met, I was unsure if I was ready to share everything because this person was a stranger. But I realized that I was at the conference and in her office because God orchestrated this divine connection and wanted me to share my story. I learned that I had baggage that I had been carrying for a long time and wasn't ready to unpack it. I began to realize that the love and encouragement that I received from my brother was what I wanted from my dad. I thought that if I didn't ask questions, then my dad would see how much I loved him because I was showing obedience. In return, he would show me the love that I wanted so badly from him. I realized in therapy that the love my father and mother showed to me was how they were shown love.

My brother started me on the journey of re-discovering my voice and having the strength to use it, but when he died, my voice died with him. The pain that started when I was young continued into my adulthood. I had to begin to break the generational curse so that I could start the healing process for myself and make sure that I didn't pass it on to my daughter. It was time to let go and start healing.

Reclaim – taking back the power in situations that once silenced you.

I have always been able to encourage others, helping them to find their voices, but to be honest, I didn't practice what I preached. I had stopped using my voice because no one listened. I was afraid to muster the courage to write my story for fear of what others would say. It was my time to be a living example of the edifying words I shared with others.

It took me until 2024 to truly start using my voice. It started with praying to God and asking Him for strength to step out in faith to begin the healing. I am learning to honor me, stand up for myself, have better relationships, and move forward in the purpose that God has designed for me. I have changed my mindset by learning to set boundaries, valuing my voice by having confidence in myself, and conquering my fears when I speak up. Since the beginning of 2024 to the present, I have been invited to speak on a panel about Type 2 diabetes, applied to become a community health influencer with the Black Women's Health Imperative, Health & Wellness program, volunteering as a mentor to three middle school girls and working on creating my non-profit. I now understand that God has designed me for a purpose bigger than I ever thought I would do. It was my journey to healing, and releasing the pain and the grief to see what He has for me. I think about my brother often and even when I do, there are tears in my eyes, but they are tears of happiness because I know that he will always be proud of his sister.

Legacy Lesson:

Wisdom is the most valuable commodity. Your gifts and talents are your wealth. Never let your age restrict you from making a difference in someone's life. Be true to yourself. Never let anyone dim your light or silence your voice. Your voice has power and will impact and inspire others.

Proverbs 4:7, ERV - *The first step to becoming wise is to look for wisdom, so use everything you have to get understanding.*

Jeremiah 29:11, ESV – *For I know the plans I have for you, declares the Lord, plans for welfare and not for evil, to give you a future and a hope.*

Live the Lesson

Reflection Page

Imagine sitting at the feet of Joyce, soaking in the wisdom she just shared in this chapter. Let her story speak to your heart as you reflect on how it connects to your own journey.

1. The Lesson that Resonates?

What moment or message in this chapter resonated with you most?

Why do you think it stood out? (Write your response below)

_____

_____

_____

2. Imagining a Conversation

With her wisdom still fresh in your mind, what's one question you would ask Joyce for further insight or clarity. Feel free to email her — her contact information is at the end of this book. *(Write your question below)*

_____

_____

_____

3. Reflection in Action

Sometimes, reflection needs to move beyond words. What is one action you can take today to honor the message in this chapter? *(Describe your action below)*

_____

_____

_____

Your Thoughts:

This is more than reflection—it's transformation in motion. Let this chapter's wisdom shape the legacy you're creating, one decision, one act, one change at a time. *(Use this space to write freely. Let your heart respond, not just your mind.)*

_____

_____

_____

Pull Back the Covers

Sheryl L. Scott

I was a little brown girl born in November 1961 and raised in the Roberts Park housing projects of Norfolk, Virginia. I was lost in a world of confusion and pain, trying to escape the trauma of what was happening to me - trauma that had been slowly eating away at me. Between the ages of six and nine is when the abuse occurred. I remember him touching me in forbidden places and making me do things to him that no child should ever have to experience at the hands of someone whom she trusted. That someone who should have been there to protect her, not to steal her innocence for his sick satisfaction and his need to control. Abuse in any form is about control, and he took total advantage and delight in what he was doing throughout those three long years.

During the time when the abuse was occurring—though I only later recognized it as abuse—my mother took me to countless doctors who ordered endless tests in search of answers. However, no one ever made the connection between the blackouts and the trauma I was enduring. No one saw that my body's way of protecting me was linked to something much deeper. But why would they? I wasn't that "fast girl" that everyone thought I was. No one suspected that the unthinkable was occurring, and I simply didn't have the words to explain it, nor did I think anyone would believe me. My subconscious was trying to shield me for as long as it could because I wasn't ready to face the ugliness of my past. The blackouts allowed me to disconnect from the world.

In my early 30s the pieces started coming together. The memories, the feelings, and those nightmares haunted me over and over again. Initially, the dreams weren't clear enough to reveal his face, but I could always see what my abuser made me do. Those visions left me with unsettling feelings, ones that made me question everything about who I was and what I could have done to warrant such an act. *Why would I dream about something like that? What was wrong with me?* I couldn't shake the thoughts and the more I tried, the more vivid they became. I was being taught a very painful lesson that would taint my relationships with men, and some women.

I remember the day that I lashed out and told my mother about the abuse. I asked her, "Why would you all not know that something was wrong with me? Why would you not question the doctors more or question why your adolescent daughter was sexually active?" She was stoic. There were no emotions shown and she didn't want to talk about it. It was like not talking about it would make it go away or it didn't happen at all. In that moment, her response (or lack of) was damaging. However, now as a mother myself, I can feel her pain of not knowing how to respond, yet wanting to bear the pain of her child. No good parent wants to see their child hurt in that way. The guilt that she must have felt because she wasn't there to protect her daughter is unimaginable.

Yes, I initially blamed her for not protecting me, even though the reality is that my mom did the best she could to provide for us—which meant working outside the home. For the majority of my younger years, she raised six children alone until she met and married again. Through therapy and God's grace and mercy, I was able to heal enough to go to her and apologize for blaming her because it was never her fault to begin with.

The confusion and shame I carried inside from the trauma left me yearning for things I didn't understand—love, acceptance, a sense of worth, a sense of belonging—and it wasn't long afterwards that I began searching for them. Searching in all the wrong places and for all the wrong things. When I was in seventh grade, I met my first boyfriend. He was two years older than me and lived at the opposite end of my street. He was the cutest boy I had ever seen—big afro, tall, and slim. All the girls in the neighborhood wanted him, but he was crazy about me. We became an item (or started "going together" as we called it back then) and I was head over heels in love. Despite having to sneak around my mom (she was strict and thought I was too young to date), we saw each other every day. His mom would allow me to visit their house as she knew that I was his girlfriend, and subsequently, I became pregnant for the first time at 14 years old.

My mother called my father, who lived in Washington, D.C., to Norfolk and they forced me to abort my baby. My boyfriend and I were devastated, but low and behold I became pregnant again a couple of months later. This time we didn't tell anyone. I continued with my daily routines, including marching with my junior high school band as I was co-captain of the majorettes. Although I was a mere 105 pounds, hiding the pregnancy was actually easy because my belly didn't protrude until I was seven months along, and even then, it just looked as though I had swallowed a basketball. My parents were disappointed, yet again, as would be any other parent who wanted the very best for their child.

Fast forward a couple of months and my baby girl had arrived. She was the most beautiful little person I had ever seen. Her jet-black hair, reddish brown skin tone, and slanted eyes reminded me of the best parts of me and her father. We doted on her so much. She was our way of showing the world that we loved each other and that out of that love we had created a life. We were determined to prove that we could be good parents even though we were young.

Being a teen mom matured me quickly. My focus was on getting an education while being the best mom I knew how to be at 15 and a half years old. My mother also was not going to have it any other way. In the beginning, she had a very hard time accepting her first grandchild, but she quickly grew to adore her. She made sure that I accepted full responsibility of taking care of my little one. Actually, her exact words were, "You did the 'adult thing' so now you're going to do the 'adult thing' and make sure that your baby is well cared for". While I knew that I had broken my mom's heart, I had the best support from her side of the family. They made sure that I would be the best teen mom ever, regardless of the circumstances.

For a while, I was enrolled in a school for pregnant teens to continue my education. My daughter's father dropped out of school and went to work full-time because he wanted to do right by us, but over time his eyes began wandering in other directions. He broke up with me shortly before my daughter's first birthday, and although we were no longer together, we still saw each other every day. His mother babysat our daughter so that I could graduate from high school.

My grades in school were excellent. I had all the credits I needed to graduate by November 1979. However, I decided to take Licensed Practical Nursing courses at Norfolk Technical Vocational Center while waiting to receive my diploma with the rest of my classmates. I think that feat surprised quite a few people, especially the busy bodies of the neighborhood who thought I'd continue to have babies and not do anything productive with my life. But that was far from the truth. You see, I now had a larger reason to push forward, as I wanted so much more for my daughter than I felt I had. It became my mission to give her that life of abundance, safe from harm, and full of love. I wasn't quite sure at the time how we would get there, but I knew we would. Despite my determination and focus, trauma found its way to reignite in my life.

After my daughter's father broke up with me, a boy I knew from junior high school started paying attention to me and I welcomed it. Since my daughter's father had walked away, I yearned for the attention he was giving to his new girlfriend. One night, the new boy asked if he could pick me up and take me for a ride and I agreed. He said that he needed to stop by his house, but we wouldn't be long because he was going to his sister's fiancée's bachelor party later that night. When we got to his house, we went to his room and began making out. Before I noticed any difference, at least three other guys had come into the room, one by one, to have their way with me. The room was dark, but it was very clear that the men were different each time. I couldn't believe what was happening, but obviously they didn't care that they were ruining my self-worth and my life.

After the last person left, I remember getting dressed and by the time my so-called friend, had come back, I was ready to go home. I said nothing the entire drive back and I never told anyone, especially not my mom. I felt everyone had already labeled me negatively and the last thing I wanted was to be viewed as easy or even worse, thinking I asked for it. Besides, I didn't think anyone would believe me or care. I never saw or heard from him again. That is until I received a Facebook friend request in the spring of 2024, over 40 years later. *How dare you!* It was the first of many thoughts that came to mind. I never responded to the request and deleted it in an attempt to burn him and decades-old disgust from my memory as I had that day back in 1981.

In November of that same year, I packed up my precious little four-year-old and we moved to D.C. to live with my father, stepmom, and two sisters. I have never regretted that decision. The city afforded us many opportunities for a better life and that was what I wanted most for my child. I dreamed of her experiencing the culture of the area and attaining as much education as she wanted as no one could take that away from her. Initially, I didn't work but rather helped care for my great-grandmother. Grandma Mary died shortly after moving in with us and I went to work full time.

In 1983, I worked in the emergency room of Capitol Hill Hospital located in northeast Washington, D.C. There I met a married paramedic who would later father my second child. He was a few years older than me and I was flattered that such a distinguished and attractive man had shown interest. He said all the right things, and because I longed to be loved, I relished in it. He could tell me that walls literally had feet and that they could walk and I would believe him. I really thought that he loved me because, unlike a married man, he spent weeks at my home. I learned many things from my relationship with him, although most of the lessons weren't beneficial. He was the first to introduce me to drugs—cocaine and marijuana. And just like that, the drug abuse began and the relationship spiraled.

I clearly remember the night my brother and dad came to my rescue when my boyfriend held a sawed-off shotgun up to my temple. We were arguing about the woman who lived above us whom he had started sleeping with. He left the apartment quickly after my dad and brother arrived. Like many who aren't yet ready to acknowledge abuse, I forgave him—and life went on. Subsequently, I gave birth to my second (and last) child, our daughter. No one could tell me anything negative about this man even though I saw him cheating. I, like so many other women, thought that I could change him because I was a good person; certainly, he would change for me even though he didn't change for his older children.

I was determined to make this piece of a "relationship" work, despite coming to work with bruises all over my arms, neck and anywhere you could think. This was not love. This was not healthy. A social worker colleague at Capitol Hill suggested that I seek treatment and I started seeing my first behavioral therapist in 1990. Sometimes, I look back and feel like a victim, but please know I AM NOT A VICTIM. I am a woman on her journey to a healthy and healed life. Therapy was a painful, positive for me. It allowed me to talk to someone who knew none of the players of my world, so no judgement could be made. I had a tendency of running when things became too difficult for me to face. My therapist had warned that my wounds would reopen and advised that I stick with therapy if I truly desired to heal.

Easier said than done. The flood gates broke open and although the revelation of being abused at such a young age was very traumatic, vivid images of the person who had initiated all this pain I was feeling came flooding in like a whirlwind. I ran out of her office and never returned. Yet, I continued searching, still trying to piece together what I thought relationships were, but I had never experienced a healthy one for comparison.

I was dating a new man at this time and he would come over after my daughters were asleep. We would get so high from smoking crack cocaine and when the first batch was gone, I gave him more money, and he'd go score more. I would say to him, "I just want the pain to stop just for a little while." But he didn't care that I was in pain nor did he care about the reason. All he cared about was that I was supplying him with drugs to get high and sex to satisfy his libido. I was hurting in a major way, and drugs and sex were the only way, so I thought, to make the voices in my head stop and the pain go away for a while. Even as I share this, my heart hurts for the person I was all those years ago, but I'm proud of the woman I've become. It was far from easy, but with God all things are possible.

In February 1997, I gave my life to God, not knowing how deeply I would need Him just two months later when my mother passed away suddenly from a massive stroke and heart attack. Losing her shattered me—she was the glue that held our family together, and her death left me feeling lost and broken. I struggled to understand why God would take her when I needed her most and found myself emotionally numb, going through the motions at work and in life. Yet, in that pain, I was drawn closer to God, leaning into prayer and scripture to find healing and purpose through the grief. Though I wrestled with doubt and didn't fully trust His timing, I kept showing up in faith, asking God to help me forgive, to carry my hurt, and ultimately, to turn my pain into something that would glorify Him.

With my head held high, I can honestly say I have been clean for over 30 years. I stopped using cocaine and marijuana. My healing had begun, but my journey was far from over. My next drug of choice became food. I ate myself to an unhealthy 274 pounds on my 5'2" frame. I would self-sabotage and eat just because I truly did not believe that I was worthy of what came, true healing, happiness, and freedom if I allowed God to have His way. Today, I am one hundred and ten pounds down and still healing. I still struggle at times with my weight, but I also know to get up from my pity party and press forward. Wanting to see my daughters and grandbaby mature to be productive citizens is worth the fight.

As I approached my 60th birthday, I noticed a significant shift in how I viewed life. I began to listen more intently to God's voice rather than the opinions of people who didn't truly understand my journey. I realized that people can be quick to offer advice, even when they haven't walked in your shoes. As I grew in my faith, it became clear that some people were uncomfortable with the changes they saw in me. Perhaps they feared my newfound confidence and independence.

When I entered my 60s, I experienced what I call my third metamorphosis. I let go of the need for approval and stopped worrying about what others thought of my choices. I started truly loving myself as the person God created and is continuing to shape. The pain and baggage of the past no longer had power over me, and I chose to focus on the wide-open future instead of the past. With clarity and purpose, I embraced the truth that I am worthy of the life God has prepared for me.

I remember waking up a few months ago to get ready for the eight o'clock service at church. I was changing the linen on my bed as I did weekly even though I had never slept on the sheets. Some might say it's strange but what a moment of healing. You see, I have never slept under the covers on my bed, whether in my own bed, family's house, or hotel. I would sleep on top of the covers and put a blanket over me. Talk about an ah-ha moment! Sleeping under the covers for me was a trigger of when my abuser would do "his business" with me or have me do things to him. Sleeping under the covers for me represented the most traumatic time in my life and I never wanted to be under the weight of the covers for fear that someone else would come in and force himself on me. This was a hurdle that I had to conquer and so that night, I pulled the covers back, climbed in, and had the *best* sleep I've ever had. I have never looked back and continue to enjoy the comforts of truly sleeping in my bed. Black eye for the devil—you no longer control me!

I have forgiven each of my abusers as I know that forgiveness is for me and not them. If I held on to the pain, the abuser would still be in control instead of me honoring God by letting Him guide me along my healing journey. Although my life has been filled with much disappointment and distress, my heart has joy knowing that God has been with me through it all and has allowed me to learn from it. I believe He has and is still using my journey to encourage me to help others who struggle with self-worth and trust after sexual, physical, and mental abuse.

My journey was truly an experience, one that I'm so very grateful to have had. No two journeys are the same and I believe that in God's infamous wisdom, He takes each of us down a different path in order to get His desired outcome. The outcome could draw you closer to Him or help you to realize your purpose. For me, it has been a combination of the two. I had to get in my head and believe that I was/am a child of God, I am who He says I am, and I belong to Him. I simply replaced negative thoughts with positive ones, which consisted of scriptures that proved His love for me. I also spoke positive affirmations like *I am a child of God, beautifully and wonderfully made in His likeness.*

Life has become calm and peaceful since I learned to get out of my own way. There have been moments when I didn't think I'd get through the day, but I really wanted to. I just needed to embrace my journey and lean into the healing. What I mean by that is deep within I felt if I let go and fully processed the trauma then I'd have nothing to complain about anymore. Well, I quickly got over that and realized that it was okay to pull the covers back, climb in, and snuggle warmly for the rest of my life. I deserve that and so much more. I now look in the mirror at the reflection staring back and there is no shame. There, looking back, is a beautiful me who has overcome a past most would not be able to endure and who has embraced a journey to get to this purpose-filled and purpose driven place. My heart is full and to have an opportunity to be transparent and honest about the mistakes I've made and be able to show little girls of all sizes, races, and backgrounds what it means to pull back those covers (layers of pain) and open up to the process of healing. If I can help one person avoid some of the same mistakes I made or avoid the craziness I faced, then every bit of the trauma would have been worth it.

Legacy Lesson:

Healing is never just about us. It's about the generations watching us—our daughters, our nieces, the little girl in the mirror who still needs to know she's worthy of love and healing. When we choose to confront our pain, we do more than find peace for ourselves—we leave breadcrumbs of courage for the ones coming behind us. So if you've ever wondered whether your story matters, let this be your reminder: your scars can be someone else's survival guide. Let them see your healing. Let them see your humanity. Let them know it's okay to break—and to *pull back the covers* to rise again.

Live the Lesson

Reflection Page

Imagine sitting at the feet of Sheryl soaking in the wisdom she just shared in this chapter. Let her story speak to your heart as you reflect on how it connects to your own journey.

1. The Lesson that Resonates?

What moment or message in this chapter resonated with you most?

Why do you think it stood out? (Write your response below)

_____

_____

_____

2. Imagining a Conversation

With her wisdom still fresh in your mind, what's one question you would ask Sheryl for further insight or clarity. Feel free to email her—her contact information is at the end of this book. *(Write your question below)*

_____

_____

_____

3. Reflection in Action

Sometimes, reflection needs to move beyond words. What is one action you can take today to honor the message in this chapter? *(Describe your action below)*

_____

_____

_____

Your Thoughts:

This is more than reflection—it's transformation in motion. Let this chapter's wisdom shape the legacy you're creating, one decision, one act, one change at a time. *(Use this space to write freely. Let your heart respond, not just your mind.)*

_____

_____

_____

Cries From the River

Dr. Patricia J. Williams

I shifted nervously in my seat, watching my daughter who sat on the floor against the airport wall. It was her last Zoom meeting before we boarded the plane to Accra, Ghana. Although she worked remotely from home, she traveled often as part of her job. I had traveled many times by plane, but this time was different. *Would I be alright?* I was excited about the opportunity to return to Africa for my second visit, but I was also full of anxiety. My first visit to Africa was a mission trip to Kimilili, Kenya. I was a healthy 61 years old, with shoulder length dark hair and no signs of arthritis. Now, I have been home from work for five weeks on family medical leave for severe arthritis pain in my knee and a pinched nerve in my hip. *How would I manage sitting for 9 hours and 36 minutes? Would I be so stiff I would need help getting out of my seat into the narrow aisle? What about those cramped airplane bathrooms? Maybe I should just try to control my thirst for the next nine hours.* These thoughts raced through my mind.

I was 73 years old traveling with young people 20 plus years younger than me and my body was far from being at its best. Finally, I settled in my mind, that no matter what, I was going to be alright. I talked to my body, *"Legs, hips, bladder, you better not embarrass me"*. I learned from my elders that sometimes you just have to talk to yourself and tell your body what to do. This was clearly one of those times.

The terminal waiting area filled up during the 3 hours we waited to board our plane. Soon, I was surrounded by a sea of black and brown people. I was a part of them, and we were all going to the Motherland—Accra, Ghana. Have you ever had a gut feeling that something different was about to happen, something you hadn't planned, but still, something good? What I didn't know was that my identity, or who I thought I was, was about to be challenged and perhaps, even changed.

We arrived in Ghana and were met by our personal driver who would be responsible for taking us to all our destinations. After stopping and unloading our suitcases at our lodging residence, we traveled to our first stop which was the President Kwame Nkruma Museum for a history lesson on the beginnings of Ghana as a nation. As we moved through the museum, I tried to put the pieces together. As a little girl, I remembered reading headlines about President Kwame Nkrumah becoming the first president of the independent nation of Ghana, but I knew very little about him. While walking through the museum, I learned more about the history of Ghana. President Kwame Nkrumah was a pivotal figure in Ghana's history. He served as Prime minister of the Gold Coast, as it was called, from 1952 until 1957. When Ghana became a republic in 1960, Nkrumah was elected as its first president. Under his leadership, a significant emphasis on economic independence led to the nationalization of the cocoa trade in 1961. He also played a pivotal role in founding the Organization of African Unity (OAU) in 1963, aiming to promote unity across the continent of Africa. Here are just a couple of his quotes that have resonated with me:

"Those who would judge us merely by the heights we have achieved would do well to remember the depths from which we started."

"I am not African because I was born in Africa, but because Africa was born in me."

I had always prided myself as being a "black American" or an "African American," but I left that museum wondering if there was even such a thing.

Next, we drove about an hour to Assin Manso Ancestral Slave River Park. This park was one of the largest slave markets during the Transatlantic slave trade, functioning as a holding site where enslaved Africans were forced to await auction. Enslaved refers to the fact that Africans were forcibly taken from their homelands against their will and transported to the Americas and other regions to be subjected to systemic exploitation and inhumane treatment as part of a brutal labor system.

When we arrived, people were walking around purchasing artifacts and listening to the drummers. After a few minutes, the drummers stopped, and the tour guide summoned us to an open-air gathering place that resembled a church with no walls. He invited us to sit on the pews. After a brief introduction about the grounds, we were asked how we felt about slavery. The tour guide waited patiently for each of us, about 50 people, to give an answer. Some said slavery made them angry, some said the whole conversation evoked sadness, others said they had no feelings at all. It had been such a long time since I thought about it. In that moment of reflection, I reflected on the replica of the slave ship in the African American Museum in Washington, D.C., as well as the slave quarters at Mount Vernon and Monticello—the fragments of history that soften the harsh reality. Yet, the true horrors of slavery—the lynchings, the brutal beatings, and the unimaginable atrocities inflicted—are often avoided and pushed aside as too painful for most of us to confront.

I was not prepared for what came next. The tour guide challenged us to change our perspective about slavery. Rather than focusing on the horrors of slavery, he challenged us to focus on the courage, the resilience, and the heart of 12 million Africans (some sources estimate as many as 16 million) who were torn from their homes and their families. He challenged us to think about the strength of the spirit of a man, woman, boy, or girl that would make them survive being branded and made to walk 400 miles in chains with little food and water, while witnessing many dying along the way with no proper burial. These were men, women, and children traumatized by horrors that are so much worse than anything that I could, or even wanted to, imagine and yet they survived.

Our transformative journey would continue down at the river. This was to be a very sacred moment when we connected with our ancestors. As I took off my shoes, I felt the sting of my age and my health issues. I was wearing compression socks, and it was going to be a lot to take them off, so I kept them on. There was also the shame of needing help to take off my socks. I didn't want my pride dampened even though I didn't know these people. After removing our shoes, we waited while each of us received a temporary white tattoo in the form of a cross on our forearm. The tattoo represented the final bath on African soil and a reminder of the atrocity of slavery. We formed a single file line and walked down to the river. The drums were silent, and we were silent. I felt a rush of emotion, sadness, fear, nervousness, anxiety. My stomach began to churn. My face felt hot. I wanted this experience, but I wasn't prepared for the wave of emotions that slowly consumed me.

With every step, I felt more anxious. This was a journey back in time. The walk to the river was a few hundred feet. The river was calm and inviting. In my head, I could hear my ancestors, mumbling in their native language, angry, and broken-hearted. Having heard stories about what happened to their brothers and sisters that were kidnapped and stolen away, they must have known their fate. The wrists of the

Africans were chained with heavy iron. An iron metal ball was attached to their feet so they couldn't run away. The enslaved Africans were only allowed to bathe in the shallowest part of the river. While the water may have offered some relief, it also likely stirred deep inner conflict. In African culture, water symbolized purification and renewal—a fresh start. For these men and women, it was a cruel reminder of their captivity, their loss of freedom, and the last bath in their homeland.

After the bath, their captors brushed their skin with the prickly leaves from the bamboo trees. Bruising the skin with the leaves forced blood to rush to the surface, gave the skin a reddish tint, and caused it to plump, making the enslaved Africans look healthier than they really were. Then they were rubbed with shea butter oil. Once they were auctioned off, they were taken to the branding station to be branded on their back, chest, or arm. I've had second degree burns that blistered my skin, but the very thought of a red, hot iron seared into my flesh made my heart race and my body shiver. Palm oil was poured on the wound to promote healing. Some of the men and women died from shock, others died trying to escape, but drowned in the water because they could not swim with the heavy iron ball on their ankles. The weaker ones were shot and their bodies dumped around the embankment on the other side of the river. This place was called "the bamboo slave dumping site". My brain was on information overload. So many details that were not in any history book or curriculum I had ever read. Granted, I didn't take a course in Black History, but shouldn't I have known about the slave river?

The tide was out, and you could almost see the bottom of the river. Some of us sat on the rocks in the water, others stood ankle deep holding hands. We all cried. I looked up at the tall bamboo trees that formed a canopy over the river. *How could such a beautiful place hold such horrendous memories?* I tried not to appear overcome by emotions, but it was so much. I was here, in history, a dark ugly history. I stood there, fixated on the water as the tears burned my cheeks and fell on my shirt. I felt for them, for their pain, hopelessness, and the shame of not being able to escape. It was here that they were stripped of their freedom, but never of their dignity. It was here that they became slaves. It was here that I felt the connection.

We gathered in small groups of four or five on the flat surface rocks in the river to complete the ceremony, "the blessing". Looking each other in the eye, searching each other's souls for the right words, we pronounced a blessing on our partners— blessings of prosperity, blessings of peace, blessings of good health, and blessings of long life. On our way out, we took pictures to capture the experience. As we exited the river, a sign above the door read, "Welcome Home." serving as a powerful symbol of the intentional return of Africans who had been dispersed across the globe.

It marked the journey of reconnection with our ancestors, finally coming back to our ancestral home.

As I climbed into the van headed for Cape Coast, a sense of relief washed over me. I reflected on my stereotypical view of Africans, often associating Africa with poverty. Even more unsettling was my narrow belief that slavery was something solely confined to Africans in America. These reflections stemmed from the societal perspectives I absorbed while growing up in the 1950's. They also highlighted the ongoing lack of awareness and teaching in modern culture about enslaved Africans, the rich history of Africa, and its modern culture.

At El Nino Cape Coast Castle, the tour guide explained that the journey from the Slave River to the castle was about 400 miles and took about 4 months. On their journey, the enslaved Africans and their captors passed through what is today called The Mole National Park. The area was filled with all kinds of wild animals including leopards, lions, antelopes, as well as many species of reptiles. The tour guide explained that to protect the captors and the enslaved Africans, the captors removed the shackles from the weakest slaves and chained them to trees. They beat their backs until blood oozed from their flesh. The animals would smell the blood and gather around the bodies to eat them. The distraction allowed the captors just enough time to pass through the park with the remaining slaves. By the time they arrived at Cape Coast, the enslaved Africans were skinny, sick, and weak.

According to Britannica Encyclopedia, during the 18th century, Cape Coast was one of several principal shipping points for the transatlantic slave trade and at any one time up to 1,500 enslaved Africans were held in the castle dungeons waiting for the next ship. It was the last place the enslaved Africans would live before leaving their homeland of Africa forever. Inside were several underground dungeons where the slaves were kept until time to board the boats to North America. We stooped down to go through the door that would take us down a narrow walkway into one of several dungeons.

The men's dungeon was a dark space with only a little window, approximately 18 feet up the wall, allowing a faint stream of light to filter. Some slaves went blind because they lived in the darkness for an extended period of time. The stone walls were cold and dark, with hollow spaces where shackles once hung. The dungeon was only meant to hold about 250 men, but usually packed with many more than that. From the back wall to the opposite wall, ran a narrow trench, about five inches wide where water continuously flowed. It was in this trench that the enslaved Africans urinated, defecated, vomited, and even bled when they could get to it. According to our guide, they were shackled in groups of four, making it difficult to get to the trench. I couldn't imagine the stench, the diseases, and the barbarity of it all.

The women's dungeon was much smaller, only built to hold about 150 women. As I walked around the women's dungeon, I thought about women delivering babies on the cold floor, blood flowing, no way to dispose of the afterbirth, so it was thrown in the trench. I thought about the smell of stale blood, puke, urine, feces—I felt sick to my stomach. It was so real, so humiliating, so disgusting. The mentally insane slaves were taken to a smaller dungeon near the back. Right above the dungeons was the church where the officers and their families sang hymns and prayed. I imagined them walking fast as they left the church to avoid the screams of insanity and pain beneath their feet. If one of the slaves died in the dungeon, they left their bodies there for days before coming to take them out and throw them into the river. Somehow, through it all, some survived, some kept their dignity.

Finally, we reached the "Door of No Return". It was a tall, narrow door. Walking through the door, there had to be a knowing that this was the last time they would touch the sand or dirt of their homeland Africa. The ships would be waiting. I stood on the shore, looking out over the ocean at the boats and people with nets full of fish. This was not what my ancestors saw. They saw ships that would take them thousands of miles away from everything and everyone they had ever known. My soul cried, though no tears left my eyes.

How did they survive? There could only be one answer. They had to survive for each other. All they had left was each other. They may not have spoken the same language, or even been from the same tribe, but they had each other.

Have you ever been to a horror movie or watched one on tv and you keep reliving the terror in your sleep and sometimes awake? On the way back to our quarters, I couldn't get the sound out of my head, the screams of hopelessness, of terror, the sight and the stench of death. But every time I heard the screams, I also heard the words, "Never forget!" I thought about their courage, their resilience, their determination to keep living. My ancestors were speaking to me, "Don't forget us!"

The next day, our travel group visited a school in Ghana, The Carolina International School. I watched as these children from ages 4 to 18 celebrated the strength and resilience of their ancestry through their enactment of the early beginnings of the transatlantic slave trade. They re-enacted the true story, including the parts where the chieftains sold their tribesmen to the British for guns and liquor. As Africans living in the United States, we know so little about the history of slavery and the resilience that is in us because of what our ancestors endured. Most of what some of us know is about plantation slavery. Sadly, most of that is from the movie "Roots" and the documentaries that run on PBS during Black History month. The history books I grew up with talked about the necessity of slaves to pick cotton and tobacco. There was a whole chapter about the plantations and slaves. Very little, if anything, was written about the enslavement of Africans brought to America. These history books were written by trained scholars, highly educated men and women who danced around the ugliness of slavery. Whether it was to avoid the true reality of the horrific atrocities of slavery, or to promote the concept of white supremacy, textbook authors wrote and passed on to generations of students, both black and white, the idea that slaves were just a part of the making of America. How can you talk about the history of America without talking about the enslavement and the denigration of Africans brought to America against their will?

My life has been changed forever. While I shed tears at the Slave River and Cape Coast Castle, my visit was not just for me to cry, to feel the pain and anguish of my ancestors, or to rehearse my hatred for what the European white man had done to my ancestors. I understand now that I am an African living in America. "I am not African because I was born in Africa, but because Africa was born in me." America is where I live, but American is not who I am. As people of color, we are not immigrants. We are the children of Africans enslaved and brought to America against their will. It was the intention of their captors to erase from their minds and hearts any connection to their homeland and it continues to be the intention of the culture of America to make Africans living in America forget our homeland, our rich history, our resilience, and our strength. Living in America, it is so easy to forget the history of how Africans were torn from their villages, their families, their homeland, enslaved and packed like sardines in a ship, only to arrive in a country that would consider them as cargo and less than a human being.

Every decade, there is less and less written for the African child living in America. No wonder we call ourselves "Black Americans", not understanding that there is no such thing. We are and will always be Africans living in America. Reading about slavery, watching movies and documentaries, and even talking about it, stirs up anger, hatred, and humiliation, however we must not get stuck in the anger. The images of the final bath, the thoughts of the punishing 400-mile trek, and the memory of the dungeon where the air had to be thick with the stench of blood, urine, and feces remains etched in my mind, bringing tears to my eyes when I think about it, even now.

Legacy Lesson:

The legacy lesson that I pass on is that we must never forget who we are, how our ancestors came to America, and what our ancestors endured, yet survived. It doesn't matter whether my ancestors came from Nigeria, Ghana, or any other African country. I am black, therefore, I am African. All these years, I never truly appreciated my ancestry. Africans were people of another country and somehow, as black Americans, we were better than them, at least that was my narrow mindedness. Despite my knowledge of the accomplishments of black people from biblical times to the present day, I still didn't appreciate my ancestry because I didn't know the story that was almost forgotten. An old African proverb says, "Until the lions tell the story, tales of the hunt will always glorify the hunter." The meaning of the proverb is that until Africans living abroad tell the true story of our ancestors, we will always live in hatred and glorify what the European white man did to us rather than glorify the dignity of our resilience and strength despite what we endured.

I boarded the plane back to America with a new determination to tell the story. During black history month, I took advantage of every opportunity to demonstrate my ancestry through my clothing. When the children in my classes commented about my African garments, I talked about Africa, my ancestors, my homeland, and their enslavement. My age and my health issues fade into the background when I think about what my ancestors endured and yet survived. All of us must tell the story, the story that brings tears running down our cheeks, makes us want to vomit, and sets our soul on fire with hatred. The story must be told by the lions. When the lion in us tells the story, we focus on our strength and our resilience. Our ancestors survived horrific trauma because they understood that all they had was each other. I encourage my African brothers and sisters not to shy away from the story, but to tell the truth, pass down the oral history of our ancestors. It is up to us to tell the story in the classrooms. We cannot allow our history to be deleted from America's history. No matter how much we thrive or survive in America, we will always be Africans living in America. When all is said and done, all we have is each other. While many of us may never have the opportunity to go home to the Motherland, we must tell the story of our ancestors and the atrocities of their enslavement both in Africa and the United States of America. Never forgetting is my silver tribute to change.

Live the Lesson

Reflection Page

Imagine sitting at the feet of Dr. Patricia, soaking in the wisdom she just shared in this chapter. Let her story speak to your heart as you reflect on how it connects to your own journey.

1. The Lesson that Resonates?

What moment or message in this chapter resonated with you most?

Why do you think it stood out? (Write your response below)

_____

_____

_____

2. Imagining a Conversation

With her wisdom still fresh in your mind, what's one question you would ask Dr. Patricia for further insight or clarity. Feel free to email her—her contact information is at the end of this book. *(Write your question below)*

_____

_____

_____

3. Reflection in Action

Sometimes, reflection needs to move beyond words. What is one action you can take today to honor the message in this chapter? *(Describe your action below)*

_____

_____

_____

Your Thoughts:

This is more than reflection—it's transformation in motion. Let this chapter's wisdom shape the legacy you're creating, one decision, one act, one change at a time. *(Use this space to write freely. Let your heart respond, not just your mind.)*

_____

_____

_____

A Journey to Knowing I'm Enough

Kim Green

It's coming back to me— as a little girl I've always longed for a dad. I always wanted a house with a white picket fence, a mom, dad, and daughter. Throughout my life, there were many auntie's boyfriends—often called 'uncle'— that came and went, but I longed for a real father figure to love me unconditionally and be my protector. Growing up in Queens, New York, it was just me and my mom until I was five. Then she met someone and that union created my sister. Finally, I had the family and security I had been searching for.

We moved to a nice home in St. Albans, Queens, where my mother, sister, and the man I now called "dad" felt like a happy family. My mother and I were always close. Watching her cook and create recipes is how I inherited my cooking skills at the age of 10. As I got older, and my brother and sisters were born, my role changed to help out with my siblings. Despite the closeness with my mother and the presence of my stepdad, there was a deeper truth I couldn't deny—I wanted my biological father in my life. I wanted to hear him tell me things like, "You're enough, just as you are" and be proud of me.

By the time I was 10, my mom and stepdad had broken up. He moved away and took my sister with him. Just like that, I lost both a sister and a dad. My heart was broken, and the sense of family and security I had was gone. As I got older, I found myself questioning why having a two-parent family mattered so much. I asked myself why my heart ached whenever I saw a father-daughter moment. Maybe it was because I wanted to feel anchored, grounded in something that was bigger than myself, and have someone who would never leave. Was I seeking validation? Or was it the need for someone to tell me I mattered?

Despite the physical absence of a father, I always felt a presence of protection around me, like someone was watching over me. I never knew my biological father because my mother never talked to me about him. When I was young, I asked her who my dad was. She would always change the subject. Sometimes, when I looked closely, I could see the sadness in her eyes, like she was carrying a burden she didn't know how to share. I wondered if she kept him locked away in the past to protect me, or maybe to protect herself. I couldn't make sense of my mother's silence. It wasn't that she didn't love me because I knew she did. But there were questions that hung in the air, unanswered… *Who was my father? What happened between them? And why was I never allowed to know?*

After my mom and step-dad broke up, we moved in with my aunt, who was the matriarch of the family. She took in other family members, as well, when they fell on hard times. She was a strong woman, that never hesitated to speak her mind. When my aunt and mother didn't see eye to eye or had a disagreement, we moved again. We moved to different areas of Southeast Queens throughout my childhood. We never stayed in one place for a long period of time and that pattern continued until I went to high school.

In the fall of 1975, I grew into a young woman and tried to push that longing for the love and affection of a father deep down inside. I envied my friends who had fathers—men who showed up to school events and games to cheer them on and who went to work each day to support their families. I still asked— *Why not me?* Did I do something wrong for my father not to be in my life? With each year that passed, I buried the questions deeper inside me. "Why didn't I have a dad?" I tried to push it aside, focusing on what I could control school, friends, the things I could make myself good at. Occasionally, like an old wound that never quite healed, the feelings would come rushing back. I had to confront it. *Why was it so important to have a father in my life?* Maybe it wasn't just about having someone to lean on. Maybe at its core, I wanted to feel seen. I wanted to know that someone cared enough to show up in my life—someone who would be there, not just when things were easy, but through the hard times too.

My freshmen year in high school was when I met my first boyfriend. He was a very popular boy on the football team. I became a cheerleader and we were inseparable. This was the first time I had got the love and the attention I was looking for. I was a teenager and no one could tell me anything, not even my mother. This was the first relationship I would start to rely on for love, comfort, and reassurance. I felt some security again, until my senior year in high school, when I came home one day, and all our belongings were in boxes outside the house. We had been evicted. I felt embarrassed, and ashamed, and an emptiness came over me causing old feelings to resurface. I tried everything to cover up my home life. I started resenting being home and resenting my mom. *Why was she letting this happen to us time and time again?* I couldn't wait to go to college and get away.

I went off to Wagner College, in Staten Island, NY, to major in nursing. I met people from all walks of life, joined organizations, and was elected student government president. I was surrounded by women with strong opinions, bold ideas, and clear goals. College was helping me grow, and through joining the local chapter of the National Council of Negro Women, I began discovering my identity and finding my voice. Going to college was the best thing I had ever done and I blossomed.

My boyfriend would come to see me while I was in college. Then one weekend, he suddenly decided to end things. My high school love of seven years broke up with me, breaking my heart to the core. I stayed in my dorm room if I didn't have to go to class. I shut myself off from friends and family, working nights so I wouldn't have to see them. I vowed never to love anyone like that again.

The breakup triggered the thoughts about my absent father to resurface and, in my twenties, I went through relationships trying to find that affection and security, again. I was never fully satisfied. Then the realization came to me one night as I was sitting alone in my room, staring out of the window. City lights outside seemed to shimmer like stars, but inside of me was stillness. I began to understand the deeper reasons behind my longing. As much as I tried to suppress it, the absence of my father left an emotional gap I could never fill. It wasn't just the idea of a "father figure" that I missed, it was the fundamental sense of being seen, supported, and validated. I realized that the absence of a father didn't mean I was broken. I had spent so many years wishing for something that was never going to be, and in doing so, I had missed the point—I was enough. I didn't need a father to make me whole.

For the first time in my life, I wasn't angry anymore. I wasn't sad, I was at peace. I didn't want to be that person anymore.

I grew into a woman with dreams, hopes, and a desire for a family of my own. I had to put on my big girl panties and get on with life. I had to go through a healing process, a love myself process. During this time, I focused on myself, I recited positive affirmations, and made plans for my future. Graduation was ahead of me and I looked forward to getting my first job. It was time to make my dreams a reality. It took a lot of self-reflection over those years to help build my self-confidence. It felt good to be self-sufficient and not look for others to make me happy and fulfilled. The pieces that I thought were missing had already been replaced by strength, resilience, and understanding that I didn't need anyone else's validation to feel complete. However, I appreciated being loved by friends, my family, and even myself. Looking back now, I understand that it wasn't about the fairy tale. It is about learning to love myself, and in doing so, finding the strength to create a life of love, connection, and meaning.

In 1985, I met my (future) husband while we were working as temporary workers for Citibank. A friendship led to dating and dating grew into love. We were married in 1987 and had twin children, a boy and a girl, in 1988. They are the joys of our lives. My daughter is definitely a girl dad, and I admire their relationship. They both love sports, especially football. She is blessed to have her dad—he is there for her no matter what. He is her protector, encourager, and the role model of qualities for her future husband. I smile when I see them together and I feel blessed that she has him as her dad. My heart no longer aches when I see a father-daughter moment, instead, I'm proud and happy. My husband is the love of my life and we've been married for thirty-seven years. I am thankful to God for the life and family that we've created.

We gave our lives to the Lord in 1995 and grew as a family in Christ. We joined ministries, learning the teaching of the Lord and the plans He had for us, which led to introducing others to Christ. I became part of a great women's ministry and I sat under some of the most prolific women preachers. I had never seen women in the pulpit before preaching God's word and about His love for us. I was a supervising chair for several years where we held annual conferences with women preachers from all over the world. Thousands of women would come to the conferences searching for answers to life's questions. They would leave filled with the Holy Spirit and the tools to equip them for the challenges life may bring.

The first time that I went to a women's conference, I witnessed a dynamic preacher and woman of God, Dr. Cynthia Hale, who's a mega-church Pastor in Atlanta, GA. Dr. Hale inspired me that day. I had never heard a woman preach the gospel like that—unapologetically, owning her role in ministry, and leading her church and community with confidence and authority. The sermon that day was titled, "A New Place in God". During this time, I gained such strength— a voice to speak up for myself and others. I realized I had a heavenly father, one who would never leave me or forsake me. When I find myself starting to feel sad, I would recite one of my favorite scriptures. Psalm 139:13-14 (NIV), *For you, created my inmost being; you knit me together in my mother's womb. I praise you because I am fearfully and wonderfully made; your works are wonderful. I know that full well.*

To this day God sustains me. He is my Father in heaven. He is my rock! I give Him all the praise. I call him when I'm in need and he provides for me. I had to always stay in the word and pull strength from scriptures that would see me through some hard times. The father I had longed for was always within me through the lessons I learned from strong women who raised me and mentored me, and through the courage to embrace who I was, without needing someone else's approval. I didn't need my biological father to be whole. I was already whole through Christ. With this strength and knowledge, I have nurtured a strong relationship with my daughter— it's special.

I have instilled in her to be her own person, to be confident, to be bold, to speak her truth. Not to hide her gifts because they are from God. To take ownership of her decisions, create goals for herself, don't let anyone else write her story, and know she can be or do anything she wants to do. She is a beautiful young lady inside and out. I didn't want her to grow up with the insecurities that I had.

I also learned to give my mother some grace. We have expectations of what our parents should be, but I had to remember that my mother was a young woman before she gave birth to me. She had hopes and dreams at one time. My mother was an aspiring artist when she was younger; years later I would see artwork she created as a teenager. Her dreams were cut short when she became pregnant out of wedlock. *How did that make her feel? Did her parents shun her? Was she ashamed? What did she give up to have me?* I had to release my mother from my expectations. I don't know how much love she received from her parents because of her situation, but she stayed and did not give me up.

Years later, my mother aspired to go to college, but she suffered a stroke. Thankfully, she pulled through, though she had to relearn how to talk and walk. I had to be there for my mom like she was there for me. I thank God now I get to have a different relationship with her, one that's full of love.

I'm thankful God gave us another chance. Now, I know who was watching over me all those years we were moving from place to place; God had a covering over our lives and a purpose and plan for me.

I am honored that through helping the old version of myself, I can help others who feel they are not good enough, smart enough, pretty enough, or bold enough.

Legacy Lesson:

My Legacy Lessons that I leave to my daughter and all the daughters out there are:

1. Have Self-Confidence

You must have a positive attitude about your abilities and skills. Understand that you are capable of doing great things. Confidence isn't about being perfect—it's knowing that you can overcome challenges and succeed. Trust in yourself and in the unique gifts you have. When you believe in yourself, others will begin to see the strength and brilliance in you. It is important to embrace who you are and never second-guess your worth. You are enough just as you are. For a long time, I had to work on this, however, I don't take it for granted the skills and knowledge I have. I am now confident in my speech, my demeanor, and appearance. If you look good, you feel good!

2. Don't Be Afraid to Shine

My daughters you are unique. God created you wonderfully and beautifully, with purpose and grace. Never hide your light or dim your spirit to make others comfortable. The world needs your individuality. Embrace your quirks, your creativity, and your mind. Stand tall in your truth and don't be afraid to stand out. There's power in owning who you are, and there is beauty in letting your authentic self shine. When I go into a meeting or an annual review at work, I shine. I enter the room confident in my worth and able to articulate what I've accomplished.

3. Believe in Yourself

You can do anything you set your mind to. Have faith in your dreams and the path you choose. Believe in the power of your actions and intentions. Surround yourself with like-minded people, who encourage you, inspire you, and remind you of your worth. Create a village of people who support you unconditionally, who will hold you accountable, and who will challenge you to grow. These are the people who will push you to be the best version of yourself because they love you and want you to succeed. I have a small circle of friends and family who support me and my goals and dreams. They hold me accountable.

4. Don't Let Anyone Define Who You Are

No one has the right to tell you who you should be or what you are capable of. You have the power. Define yourself and set your own boundaries. Don't let society, your peers, or anyone else's expectations shape your identity. Challenge yourself to step outside your comfort zone, try new things, and explore things that you never thought possible. Whether it's joining a class, picking up a new hobby, or going to social events, push yourself to grow and experience life to the fullest. You are the architect of your future. Over the years, I have learned to push myself out of my comfort zone by doing things like traveling and going to events alone. When I go to places where I don't know anyone, I welcome the challenge of getting to know new people.

5. Love Yourself Before You Can Love Anyone Else

Self-love is essential to living a fulfilling life. Before you can give love to others, you must first give it to yourself. Be kind to yourself during times of struggle and take time to celebrate your victories, big or small. Learn patience with yourself as you grow, change, and evolve. Embrace your journey and always remember that growth is a process. You deserve your own love, care, and respect, and you are worthy of them. Over the years I have grown to love and be kind to myself. I don't beat myself up if I don't get something right the first time. I give myself grace.

6. Keep God First

My Beloved, always keep God first in your life. Welcome Him into your heart, and trust in his guidance. Staying close to God will give you the strength and wisdom you need to navigate through life's trials and tribulations. He will help you find your purpose and direction when you feel lost or uncertain. Read His word daily and lean on it when life gets tough. His love will carry you through, and it will never fail. Remember, you are never alone, for He is always with you. My faith is what sustains me. I love God truly— He is Abba, my father. I am a servant of Him through participating in ministries at my church that serve His people.

Legacy is defined as the positive impact your life has on others—whether they're friends, colleagues, or even strangers. It's the sum of your personal values, accomplishments, and actions that leave a lasting impression on those around you. I'm honored to share this chapter of my life's journey with you. I hope that in doing so, it resonates with someone, inspires them, and reminds them they are not alone. We all have stories to tell, even if we don't always realize it. Then, someone comes along who sees the story within you and helps you dig deep to share it. If my story inspires even one person, my purpose is fulfilled.

Live the Lesson

Reflection Page

Imagine sitting at the feet of Kim soaking in the wisdom she just shared in this chapter. Let her story speak to your heart as you reflect on how it connects to your own journey.

1. The Lesson that Resonates?

What moment or message in this chapter resonated with you most?

Why do you think it stood out? (Write your response below)

_____

_____

_____

2. Imagining a Conversation

With her wisdom still fresh in your mind, what's one question you would ask Kim for further insight or clarity. Feel free to email her—her contact information is at the end of this book. *(Write your question below)*

_____

_____

_____

3. Reflection in Action

Sometimes, reflection needs to move beyond words. What is one action you can take today to honor the message in this chapter? *(Describe your action below)*

_____

_____

_____

Your Thoughts:

This is more than reflection — it's transformation in motion. Let this chapter's wisdom shape the legacy you're creating, one decision, one act, one change at a time. *(Use this space to write freely. Let your heart respond, not just your mind.)*

_____

_____

_____

Reconnected: A Legacy Forged in Courage, Reconciliation, and Rediscovery

Sybil Perry

Adam was lonely in the Garden of Eden before God made him a companion; somebody to help and compliment him. "She is bone from my bone", declared Adam. God's will is still for a wife to be the helpmate for her husband and stand by him no matter what.

"Divorce is not the problem. The problem is defective marriage, due to defective individuals who come together outside of the "garden" context-people who have never become truly single." (Dr. Myles Munroe, 2003)

When a woman says "yes" to a marriage proposal, she agrees to join her life with the man pursuing her, talking with her, spending time with her, and, sometimes, living with her. I never would have said "yes" if I had known there would be times when my future husband would stop romancing me, spend more and more time away for work or play, and begin to take second glances at other women. Reflecting on my marriage and why I am still with my husband 43 years later, I recognize how God has kept me in His Perfect Peace. He preserved my well-being as far back as I can remember, as evident in the timing of various challenges and my answered prayers. It was all necessary for this new, successful marriage we have today.

My husband and I met in the US Navy in 1981. Before I joined the Navy, I was working as a medical assistant for an OB-GYN provider and wanted to become a nurse. One day, I was walking on my lunch break and saw a sign that led me into a Navy recruitment office. I spoke with the recruiter and was briefed on the benefits and travel that the Navy offered. Those opportunities sounded great, including being able to simultaneously pursue a career in the medical field. I wanted to follow in the footsteps of my mother, who also worked in healthcare. When I went home to inform her of my decision, she asked, "What are you running away from?" In my eyes, I wasn't running away. I was intentionally pursuing what felt like the beginning of my purpose journey, even if I couldn't fully articulate it at the time.

On July 11, 1980, I left my hometown of Atlanta, Georgia, and headed to the United States Navy boot camp in Orlando, Florida. It lasted for 8 weeks, during which I jogged, did push-ups and sit-ups, and became athletically fit. Although I was physically fit, there were times when my mental space was challenged—especially when I faced what felt like petty punishments or when my personality clashed with the strict demands of military authority. One time, a drill instructor got so close I instinctively looked up, which she interpreted as eye-rolling, and I was disciplined for it. I graduated from boot camp in October 1980 and transferred to Great Lakes, Illinois, for Hospital Corpsman (HM) Training. There I learned to assist healthcare professionals in providing medical and dental care to Navy and Marine Corps personnel and their families, as well as performing other duties that aided in the prevention and treatment of disease and injury. As a clinical technician, medical administrator, and healthcare provider, I was responsible for administering emergency care, sometimes in combat zones. After this 8-week training, I traveled to my first duty station at a Naval hospital in Beaufort, South Carolina. When I arrived, I thought, "Wow, what a small town!" As a city girl, I didn't think I would survive there — *where were the malls?*

One day as I was checking in at the command center, I noticed a young man walking down the hall. He was handsome, had nice wavy hair, and the way he looked in that black Navy uniform made me feel an immediate spark of pleasure, and curious about the possible reward of being with him. I wanted to meet him. Some of my colleagues noticed my interest, as my facial expression was obvious to them, and they decided to arrange a meeting without informing me. We met, briefly, conversed with small chit-chat, and then went our separate ways. A few months later, we saw each other again and talked more, which led to a first date. More time spent together led to officially dating after around six months. Then, external influences began to affect our relationship.

Other women were also interested in him and attempted to pursue him. One woman even approached me to claim he belonged to her and suggested I stay away. I asked if that was a threat and she confirmed it was. I decided that competing for his attention was not worth fighting for. Yet, he thought otherwise, and we decided to continue our relationship. This led to moving out of the barracks and into our own apartment.

In December 1981, we got married and on January 18, 1982, we were blessed with a beautiful baby boy. Afterwards, my husband was deployed and I was home for 6-8 months with our son. During the times when my husband and I both had to deploy, I would have to take our son to Atlanta for my mother to care for him. Our house was peaceful when we were both stationed at home because we had never been together for more than a year at a time. For example, my husband left Beaufort for Field Medical Training in Hawaii. I was left in Beaufort, and when I finally received orders to be with him, my son and I traveled to Hawaii. However, he was already ship-bound and deployed to another location. I was blessed with a sponsor who picked up my son and me from the airport, helped us obtain and settle into our new home, arranged daycare for my son, and helped me prepare for duty at my new command.

It was hard being away from family, however I stayed in contact with my mother. We chatted daily, took virtual cooking lessons, and I received updates on family matters, which kept me connected to what was going on in Atlanta. My mother and I were so close—she was my best friend. When she unexpectedly passed away in September 1996, I was devastated—it almost took me out. Due to my grief, I was unable to return to Maryland and was in Atlanta well over the time allotted for leave. I still miss her, and to this day, I have gone up to the phone to call her, only to remember that she's gone.

As challenging as those times were, being deployed away from family, God kept my husband and me stationed in the same city and state, yet not at the exact location. Being stationed onboard a ship and having to deploy away from my husband and son was not something I was happy about, yet here we go again, another separation, sometimes up to 6-9 months at a time, and this happened throughout our Navy career for the first 10-12 years of our marriage. Marriage—a sacred union of commitment that I believe neither of us fully understood.

I think there was infidelity at the forefront of our marriage. The sneaky, distant behavior and not knowing any of his, supposedly, platonic "girlfriends", made it challenging to understand these female relationships that we did not share. There was an emotional connection with a specific woman that I just did not understand and no matter how much I expressed my dissatisfaction, this relationship still meant so much to him. She was his "best friend", who he conversed with often. I didn't know her, but she knew all about me. We could never go around her as a couple, nor could he talk to her on the phone around me. A man and woman being best friends, without an emotional attachment...*yeah, right.* Their relationship was purposefully hidden, so I didn't believe it was innocent. During this time, there were a lot of distant feelings and disconnection between my husband and I, so what was I supposed to think?

These, what I refer to as intimate conversations between them, may have been innocent initially, but the emotional bond grew stronger over time, and eventually, she expressed her feelings for him. And guess what? She was married too! My husband revealed that to me and continued to state she was just a "friend". We argued about this relationship often, and yet they remained friends until I had truly had enough. I believe talking about their shared experiences contributed to their stronger emotional connection. *How dare he continue to talk to her and open up to someone who was a factor in the daily stresses of our marriage.*

Then I began to think, *maybe I should have a male friend/confidante as well.* Though I was not actively seeking an opportunity, I was approached romantically by another Navy colleague of mine and decided to retaliate by becoming physical with him while I was away from home on a deployment. It was a big mistake, and I immediately knew that was not the answer. I never saw the man again, yet he did contact me upon returning from deployment, and my husband saw the email of him wanting to see me again. My husband's reaction was as if a world war had begun. He, surprisingly, became extremely angry and refused to forgive me, stating how I had continually accused him for years, and how dare I go and do something like that. Then he moved out of our home—and had an affair with his co-worker.

Our separation was a time for self-reflection and self-development, as I prepared for divorce. There were feelings of inferiority and blaming myself for the failure of the marriage. I began to look inwardly at my personality and became realistic about my strengths and weaknesses. I realized that my resilience and drive were undeniable strengths, but I also had a tendency to shut down emotionally when I felt vulnerable. I also found that I had put all the blame on him, yet had not looked within to see the offenses I had committed. What things had I contributed to this devastation and allowed to creep into my heart and fester? Even in my anger, I continued to pretend I was okay but still thinking thoughts of mistrust and what-ifs. This was an uncomfortable weight to carry day to day. This self-evaluation allowed me to begin personal growth and, more importantly, concentrate on my relationship with God by seeking and learning to serve Him.

Dealing with shattered trust, heart turmoil, outright pain, and low self-esteem was a stressful experience. There were so many lessons learned throughout this process. First, I would say when there is a disagreement between a husband and wife, it opens a door for Satan to gain a foothold in the marriage. It takes great wisdom to resolve conflicts promptly. My husband and I would reconcile on issues, yet unforgiveness and heartache were still present. Instead of dealing with the infidelity by either leaving or seeking counseling, we stayed together, sweeping things under the carpet, harboring anger and unforgiveness, which led to lashing out and more distance which solved nothing.

You cannot bring outsiders of a different sex into an already challenging situation. They may act ready to listen and show sympathy for the struggles you discuss with them, and then offer a shoulder to say, "You know, if I were married to you, I definitely wouldn't treat you that way." *Really?* You must question and/or discern what are their true intentions.

Commitment, respect for one another, and trust were lessons we both learned as events unfolded. There was growing emotional distance in our marriage that eventually pushed us to the brink of separation in 2001, with the thought of divorce hanging heavily in the air. We separated, and through various conversations, the challenges of being separated, yet still married brought on their distractions of uncertainty for both of us.

In 2002, the turning point came when we both realized we truly loved each other, and our marriage was worth fighting for. We finally sat down and poured out our hearts, sharing the pain, loneliness, and desire for the connection we both longed for. Realizing we had been neglectful in our ways toward each other, we both knew there was a genuine desire to stay together and reconcile our marriage.

As we began to rebuild, I still had emotions of anger and uncertainty. I didn't know if I had made the right decision to return and try, or if I could really move past what I thought was the worst thing ever—infidelity in a marriage. Yet, it wasn't my decision to make; it was a word from God that propelled me into doing what I was purposed to do. Out of it all, there was one thing I did know: I loved my husband, I loved God more, and obedience was better than sacrifice. So, I began to do the work for my marriage that was required of me—praying, fasting, and seeking God's guidance. Could I truly forgive and live with him for the rest of our lives as husband and wife?

Really Sybil? You are a high school and college graduate, you have spent 22 years in the United States Navy, retired, honorably, a wife of 43 years, a mother, a grandmother, and most of all, a daughter of the Highest King of Kings, who without Him, you would not have been able to achieve any of those accomplishments while still going through the difficult seasons in your marriage.

I thank God today (2025) for my husband and all he does for us, for allowing us to grow and learn to love each other even more, and for enabling us to work through and grow as we are in our fourth decade of marriage. God did that; it was necessary to make us better people for each other and others. As I have matured in my faith and completely forgiven those who have betrayed me, removed my hands from things that are not mine to handle, and let God do the work in me, all things are working for my good.

Legacy Lesson:

I share this story to say that divorce is not always the answer. I have many friends who say that infidelity is a game-changer and will not be tolerated. I can agree in some instances. Yet, we never know what we would do until we have been put in a situation. Through the challenges in my marriage, I compensated well by always covering and not being transparent about what I was feeling. That took me down a path of lashing out and carrying the hurt and shame until I finally realized that nothing or no one is perfect and how to be transparent about who I am and how I feel. I had to remove judgment not only of my husband but also of myself.

This life experience, like others, has matured me and shaped my involvement in this challenge. I had to genuinely forgive, my husband and myself, learn the lessons, and realize I could not change anyone or manage anything on my own. I began to do the work, to dig deep, cry, share, and allow God to continue the work that He started from within. I stayed in prayer and watched God do His thing. I prayed for truth and came to realize the beauty of the gospel. I learned that others do not define my identity, but by who I am in Christ. Jesus tells me I am loved, accepted, and valuable. God has used my challenges and experiences to shape me, growing my compassion, resilience, structure, and hope. He has turned my challenges into blessings for His glory.

My husband and I share a love that has never been stronger. By acknowledging our mistakes, offering forgiveness, and expressing genuine love, we continue this journey together.. There is more respect and emotional intimacy, allowing us to be ourselves without fear of judgment. I understand that God has put us together for His purpose, not perfection, and we have reason to believe that what God promises is a commitment we can rely on. God gives us counsel for spiritual, natural, and practical matters; His counsel is made available for everything we go through. God's counsel will shift you from the path you think you should be on and take you to a place of love and compassion. Some of my friends divorced, and I thought, *See…if I would have just left*, then God said, "No—that is not the path I have for you."

When we dwell in anger, we are not partnering with God. I felt entitled to my anger, and yet, as a believer, I must view things through God's perspective and respond differently. Every married couple may encounter some form of frustration, hurt, unfulfilled expectations, unrealized dreams, and unhappiness during their relationship. Our response to these disappointments can mature us and draw us closer to God and to one another, or we can let these setbacks destroy us and our marriage.

As long as the relationship is safe and free from abuse or danger, fight for your marriage. With wisdom, self-assessment, forgiveness, and the right tools for reconciliation, love can be restored. Healing is possible, and so is rediscovery.

Live the Lesson

Reflection Page

Imagine sitting at the feet of Sybil soaking in the wisdom she just shared in this chapter. Let her story speak to your heart as you reflect on how it connects to your own journey.

1. The Lesson that Resonates?

What moment or message in this chapter resonated with you most?

Why do you think it stood out? (Write your response below)

_____

_____

_____

2. Imagining a Conversation

With her wisdom still fresh in your mind, what's one question you would ask Sybil for further insight or clarity. Feel free to email her—her contact information is at the end of this book. *(Write your question below)*

_____

_____

_____

3. Reflection in Action

Sometimes, reflection needs to move beyond words. What is one action you can take today to honor the message in this chapter? *(Describe your action below)*

_____

_____

_____

Your Thoughts:

This is more than reflection—it's transformation in motion. Let this chapter's wisdom shape the legacy you're creating, one decision, one act, one change at a time. *(Use this space to write freely. Let your heart respond, not just your mind.)*

_____

_____

_____

The Value of a Relationship Coin

Jackie Togun

I have spent most of my life placing more value on my life's goals than my life's relationships. I was hiding behind my achievements, convincing myself it was a safe place to be—because I didn't yet know my value. Over years of reflection, I discovered the rare and unique qualities that make me who I am and how God showed me purpose through the relationships I had with others. It first began with my mother.

Lena Mosby—sunrise May 2, 1927, in Halifax County, Virginia. One of seven children born to Ned and Carrie Hodges. She was a tiny woman with short, curly black and gray hair (we gray early in our family). Her gorgeous, high cheekbones were inherited from her great-grandmother, who was Native American—either Sappony or Cherokee. My mother had a unique smile. When she smiled, it seemed like she was "up to something," yet fully enjoying whatever moment she was in. Sometimes she would chuckle about something and if it was really funny, she danced a "short jig". Momma's joyful childhood moments were dimmed when she was separated from her siblings because her father was murdered. Then shortly after, her mother died from an illness. Momma didn't talk much about her past, but when it came to her father's death, I remember her mentioning an incident where a man was flirting with one of her sisters, and her father confronted him. That altercation ended with his murder.

After her parents' deaths, Momma went to live with a family that had a disabled son. Although she was very young, she became a live-in maid and caregiver for their son. The work was far from easy. Each day began before dawn — she was the first to rise, tasked with starting fires in the wood stoves. She walked miles to draw water from a well. Once she recalled being so sick with a high fever and painful boils on her forehead, yet she was still expected to carry out all of her duties. She cooked their meals and even had to light and help smoke cigarettes for their son. The way Momma described it, she would light his cigarette, take a few puffs herself, and then place it on his lips. Her steady hand supported each puff that he took. This marked the beginning of her becoming a life-long smoker.

When she was old enough to be on her own (probably between 16 and 18 years old), she left this family and was reunited with her siblings. It was during this time in her life that, she met my father. Although there was a big difference in their ages, she decided to marry him. For several years she wanted to get pregnant, but couldn't. Finally, she did and I was born. Her prayer was to have children and she did — 10 of us! It would have been 12, but she had 2 miscarriages. I was my mother's built-in babysitter and helper. Growing up, our relationship was mostly about getting things done to maintain the household.

I grew up in rural Henrico County, Virginia. We had a well for water, an "out-house" and an inside "pee-pot" for bathroom use, and a round metal tub for baths. We had two wood stoves—one in the area used for our kitchen and one in the living room. Our washing machine consisted of a tub-like base with an upper wringer attached to it. We had two medium-sized bedrooms upstairs with a small room (half the size of one bedroom) in the middle. This room had one small window and a tiny closet. It was just big enough for a twin-size bed and a small table. Momma gave this room to me. That left her and my father to sleep in one bedroom and the rest of my siblings in the other. I considered this little room to be a special gift. It was in this same room that I fell asleep and dreamed of Jesus knocking at the door. When I let Him in, a powerful sensation swept over my body, woke me up, and I quickly sat up in bed. This was my first encounter with the presence of Jesus in my life.

Looking back, I believe that encounter was preparation for the obstacles I would face in life and what would keep me going. Especially after the death of my mother. Lena Mosby—sunset May 21, 2013. After many years of battling bipolar disorder and depression, diabetes, and heart disease, Momma left us to mourn her departure. She died a widow because her second husband had died several years before. My parents divorced when I was in the middle of my teenage years. My father went on to live a life without us and died from heart and lung disease when I was in my early 20s.

Years after my mother's death, I was able to connect the dots concerning her emotional, mental, physical, spiritual, and social journey. I can't recall us having any "girly girl" moments, long intimate conversations, or time spent laughing about something that was funny to both of us. But occasionally, she would share important etiquette nuggets like, always walk on the right side, if you're on a sidewalk, on stairs, or in a hallway. When you enter a room of people, always speak; and if someone gives you something, be grateful. In life, some things may not look (or sound) like much from the outside, but can turn out to be internal (and external) treasures. I carry Momma's wisdom nuggets with me to this day. Like finding a rare coin, I was able to examine her life and realize how valuable her story is. I found lessons in her childhood, her relationship with her siblings, and her marriages. Thinking about the small circle of people she called friends and how deeply she cared for family—even our children—I realized I could have done more, been there for her more, and loved her more.

Around but not around, helpful but not helpful, communicating but not really communicating. Over time, this became the relationship with my mother. This relationship felt okay because my energy and attention were focused on accomplishing things in my own life. Around the time I was ready to graduate from high school, I had met someone and we started dating. In the span of two years, I graduated from high school, completed an 18-month nursing program, and was married. My husband was in the Army. Soon after we married, he was deployed to Korea. I wanted very much to go with him, but he decided that I shouldn't. So, I stayed, started a career as a Practical Nurse, and was living on my own as a newlywed. I was away from my mother and siblings, but aware of a lot that was going on with them. I was aware, but not connected.

Within three years, my husband returned from Korea, we had two children, and eventually got a divorce. We were both in our early 20s. Although we talked about our future, we had different thoughts about how to actually get there. In the midst of me getting pregnant with our first child, his attention was not on our new baby that was on the way but, on buying a new car and spending a lot of time with his friends. Time with his friends resulted in a woman's phone number being found by me, in one of the pockets on a pair of his pants that I was getting ready to wash. He claimed that there was "nothing to it" but, for me, it was the beginning of distrust in our marriage; that eventually led to our divorce.

I found out many years later from one of my siblings that when I decided to get married it was a very sad time for my mother. She never told me how she felt and I never talked to her about it. I suppose some of her tears were because I didn't have a clue about the results of my decision to get married. I regret that my mother and I didn't or couldn't have that conversation. As a result, I continued looking for love in all the wrong places.

After five years of dating a man from Nigeria, we married only for it to end in what would be for me, a second divorce. He had another family here in America. I had to endure the drama created by that situation until his secret family, escorted by him, went back to Nigeria. He came back to America and we spent five years as husband and wife; taking care of four children. By this time, I had a daughter and a son who were born out of our relationship. This time around the divorce table was more devastating for me because I believed that he truly loved me and my children and that he would provide a happy future for us. Two divorces and four children later, I told God, "I'm tired". My heart and soul cried out for me to make a change.

On a Sunday morning, I got up, got dressed, and went to a church near the apartments where I lived. During the altar call, while the choir sang "Blessed Assurance", I heard an inner voice say, "You better go up now!" That day, I made a choice and God made the change. I would begin a journey that would include God's sovereignty, God's truth, and God's plan. This change would include years of seeking God's will for my life. I was in Sunday morning worship, bible study, and working in the church wherever I could help. I was also spending more time on personal study and prayer. In my pursuit of successful single parenting, I created 'Because You're Special (BYS)' moments with my children.

These were days I tried to give each of them individual time and attention. However, because of my schedule and many times having no extra money, BYS days went out the window.

My finances got worse—to the point of homelessness. My children and I had to sleep on mattresses in an extra bedroom at a friend's house and feel the discomfort that came when our welcome there was worn out. There was a time I had to heat our bedroom from the oven in the kitchen nearby and cover ourselves with coats to make it through the night. Even though those arrangements weren't always the best, I thank God for the family and friends who took us into their homes. I had yet to realize that this experience was part of the change that God would use to restore me and it wouldn't always feel good.

Change would include having to transition from one job to another. Even though I spent many years acquiring academic success, the career that I was professionally trained for, a Christian School Administrator, was never fully realized. I know what it feels like to get a "pink slip" (more than once); to go to cash a check and the money from the company I work for not be there; to be "black-balled" for something I said, while being given a wonderful farewell party.

Church hurt was also a part of my change. As a young Christian, I became a member of a church that welcomed me with "open arms". Yet, I felt a lack of connection, fellowship, and support from some leaders and the people connected to them. This left me with a broken heart for many years. Along with wounds from my romantic relationships that ended with multiple broken marriage proposals.

There were so many times when God said, "Go right" and I went left. The regret and sadness of these times is that I thought I was right. But, as one wise man has said, "You can be sincere but, sincerely wrong". My change had its share of sorrows, sufferings, and afflictions but, the good news is that it has not been void of God's presence, His power, His promises, His protection, His provision, His peace, and His prosperity. God's love gave me the ability to walk through times of change, in His strength, to be able to get to where I need to go. For me, this journey has included being able to understand and embrace "truths" that yield the healing and freedom that God wants for me as His daughter.

Only God's grace and mercy and His willingness to increase my understanding has allowed me to see relationships through a different lens. From the very beginning, God's love for us sparked His desire to have a relationship with us. He gave us His blueprint via His word, The Holy Bible. His expectations were communicated through His requiring us to first, love Him with all of our being. He already knew that as we loved Him back, His love for us would cause us to not only be able to experience self-love, but also to have the capacity to love others correctly. This God kind of love is demonstrated through relationships, that because of connection, communication, and community, create healthy interactions; where those who are linked together are thriving, valuing one another and providing for each other a support system that, cultivates a sense of wellbeing.

When this blueprint for relationship is absent, dysfunction is the result. Sometimes we lack the ability to have healthy relationships because of our environment; situations where nobody knows how, or "models" how God wants to do relationships. Sometimes dysfunction is present because of the choices we make; choices where we know what's right to do but, we do what we really want to do, anyway. At any rate, someone has said, "When you don't know the purpose of a thing, abuse is inevitable." And so, here I am. Taking a deep breath. Feeling sad and regretful that I messed up so bad, but, rejoicing that God loves me anyhow. I truly understand as someone has said, "The script could have been written another way." I could be dead from a sexually transmitted disease. I could be living physically disabled as a result of jumping out of a moving car to keep from being raped. By now, I could be sitting somewhere not knowing my name or what day it is. BUT GOD! Instead, I am sharing this with you.

Legacy Lesson:

Life here on earth as we know it is too short to miss opportunities to have valuable and rich relationships;

relationships where we are *present*, loving, communicating, and sharing. This may look very different for each relationship, but take the time to discover the rarity and the priceless value of each person given to you on this journey we call life. Ascribing value is important because it is a vantage point from which we can prioritize, enrich, nurture, honor, and support those around us. Someone has said, "Take time to smell the roses". I invite you to take time, wherever you are on your life's path, to value your relationships. I have had to accept the fact that, there are people in my life that deserve more of my attention simply, because of the rarity of their presence. As a mother, grandmother, great-grandmother, sister, auntie, friend, servant leader, co-worker, neighbor, etc., I can do better! I plan to be more intentional about creating "rare moments"; moments that say, "I love you. I appreciate you. I affirm you. I celebrate you!" I am now spending time looking at my resources, my weekly schedule, and prioritizing who I need to spend time with. I am also examining what time spent with the people in my life should "uniquely" look like. I have been talking to my sisters and brothers, hoping that, we'll be able to spend some time together soon. Remember, it all starts with putting God first. Please do it—you'll be glad that you did. Finally, as you carve out more intentional moments of gathering valuable coins, remember this: In the currency of legacy, few investments yield greater returns than the ones we make in people. Relationships—nurtured with time, trust, and truth—become sacred spaces where transformation takes root and blossoms. The relationship coin is more than a sentimental token; it is a timeless deposit into the souls of those we love, lead, and live alongside.

Let this be your charge: Spend your relationship coin wisely. Sow it into meaningful connection, not convenience. Trade it not for approval, but for authenticity. Let it reflect who you are and who you are becoming. Because when the silver of your years begins to shine, and your words become whispers of wisdom passed down, may it be said that your greatest wealth was not what you left behind—but *who* you left better.

Keep investing. Keep connecting. Keep changing—and watch your legacy multiply.

Live the Lesson

Reflection Page

Imagine sitting at the feet of Jackie soaking in the wisdom she just shared in this chapter. Let her story speak to your heart as you reflect on how it connects to your own journey.

1. The Lesson that Resonates?

What moment or message in this chapter resonated with you most?

Why do you think it stood out? (Write your response below)

_____

_____

_____

2. Imagining a Conversation

With her wisdom still fresh in your mind, what's one question you would ask Jackie for further insight or clarity. Feel free to email her—her contact information is at the end of this book. *(Write your question below)*

_____

_____

_____

3. Reflection in Action

Sometimes, reflection needs to move beyond words. What is one action you can take today to honor the message in this chapter? *(Describe your action below)*

_____

_____

_____

Your Thoughts:

This is more than reflection—it's transformation in motion. Let this chapter's wisdom shape the legacy you're creating, one decision, one act, one change at a time. *(Use this space to write freely. Let your heart respond, not just your mind.)*

_____

_____

_____

Additional Legacy Lessons to Learn and Live

Perhaps after reading the chapters in this book, you found yourself pressing gently against the walls of your cocoon—ready to emerge, yet still sensing there's more to gather before your wings fully unfold. That's the thing about transformation: it doesn't happen all at once. It happens in layers, in lessons, and in legacy.

You've sat at the feet of wisdom. You've been wrapped in the stories of women who poured their journeys into the pages. But maybe, just maybe, something in your soul is still stretching, still seeking, still whispering, *"Give me more..."*

So here they are—more silver pieces of change.

Legacy lessons, unearthed like sacred treasures, offered to you like morning dew resting on the edge of a new beginning. These truths aren't just to be read—they are to be lived. These aren't just words—they're wings, meant to carry you further along your metamorphosis.

Take what you need. Leave what no longer serves you. But by all means—**keep growing**.

1. **The Power of Resilience**
   Lesson: Life will always throw challenges our way, but it's not the difficulties that define us—it's how

we respond to them. Resilience comes from finding strength even in moments of uncertainty.

Legacy: Don't be afraid to fall, because it's in getting back up that you'll discover your true strength.

2. **The Importance of Staying Curious**
   Lesson: The world is always changing, and maintaining a curious mindset is the key to growth. Ask questions, explore new ideas, and never stop learning.
   Legacy: Keep your curiosity alive—there is always more to know, and it's never too late to learn.

3. **Embrace Imperfection**
   Lesson: Perfection can be a trap that holds us back. It's our flaws and mistakes that make us human, and often they are the source of our greatest lessons.
   Legacy: Don't strive for perfection; instead, embrace the beauty in imperfection. It's where life's true magic often lies.

4. **The Value of Patience**
   Lesson: In a world that prizes instant gratification, learning patience can be one of the most valuable tools. Things take time, and the best things often come when we're willing to wait.
   Legacy: Remember, good things take time. Patience doesn't mean inaction; it's the quiet trust that everything will unfold as it should.

5. **The Strength in Vulnerability**
   Lesson: Showing vulnerability is not weakness but an act of bravery. True connections and growth happen when we allow ourselves to be seen for who we really are.

   Legacy: Don't be afraid to show your true self—your vulnerability can be a bridge to deeper, more meaningful connections.

6. **Cherish Relationships Over Material Wealth**
   Lesson: At the end of the day, it's the people in your life who matter most. Build relationships with care, and focus on love and respect, not just on accumulating wealth.

   Legacy: Money and possessions fade away, but the relationships you nurture will last a lifetime.

7. **The Importance of Forgiveness**
   Lesson: Holding onto anger or grudges only hurts ourselves. Forgiveness is not just for others—it's a gift we give ourselves to move forward with peace and clarity.

   Legacy: Forgiveness is freeing. Don't carry the weight of past hurts—it only holds you back.

8. **Taking Risks**
   Lesson: Sometimes, the greatest opportunities lie just beyond our comfort zones. Take calculated risks, and don't be afraid to venture into the unknown.

Legacy: The greatest regrets often come from the chances we didn't take. Don't be afraid to step into the unknown.

9. **Mindfulness and Living in the Moment**
   Lesson: In today's fast-paced world, it's easy to overlook the beauty of the present moment. Taking the time to pause and truly experience life can lead to more fulfillment.
   Legacy: Don't rush through life. Pause, breathe, and take in the moment. It's in the present that you'll find true happiness.

10. **The Importance of Giving Back**
    Lesson: Life is not just about what we can get, but what we can give. Helping others, whether through time, resources, or kindness, brings fulfillment and meaning to our lives.
    Legacy: It's not what you take, but what you give that leaves a lasting legacy.

11. **Understanding the Value of Time**
    Lesson: Time is the one resource we can never get back. Use it wisely—focus on what truly matters, and don't waste it on things that don't serve your well-being or dreams.
    Legacy: Time is precious. Spend it on what brings you joy, growth, and connection, and let go of what drains you.

12. Creating a Legacy Through Actions

Lesson: Our legacy is not built through words alone, but through the things we do. Your actions, big and small, leave a mark on the world.

Legacy: Your legacy is not just in what you say, but in what you do. Make every action count.

13. Living Authentically

Lesson: Don't waste your life trying to fit into someone else's mold. The most fulfilling life is the one where you embrace your true self, flaws and all.

Legacy: Live authentically—be yourself, unapologetically. It's the only way to live fully.

14. Appreciating the Simple Things

Lesson: The most meaningful moments often come from the simplest experiences. Take time to appreciate the small joys in life, like a sunset or a good conversation.

Legacy: Sometimes the greatest beauty lies in the simplest moments. Take time to appreciate them.

15. Living with Gratitude

Lesson: Focusing on what you have, instead of what you lack, shifts your mindset and creates a more positive, fulfilled life.

Legacy: Gratitude is the key to happiness. When you appreciate what you have, life becomes richer.

16. Finding Peace in Solitude

Lesson: In a world filled with distractions, taking time for solitude allows you to reconnect with yourself, your thoughts, and your purpose. Embrace moments of quiet for reflection and growth.

Legacy: Solitude is not loneliness. It's an opportunity to hear your own heart and find the answers that lie within.

17. The Power of Kindness

Lesson: Kindness doesn't cost a thing, yet it can change someone's day, or even their life. Small acts of kindness create ripple effects that improve the world around us.

Legacy: Never underestimate the power of a simple act of kindness. It's the smallest gestures that can make the biggest difference.

18. Adaptability in Times of Change

Lesson: Change is inevitable, and how we respond to it determines our success and happiness. Embrace change with an open heart and mind, knowing that growth often comes from the unexpected.

Legacy: The world changes, and so must we. Embrace change, and you'll discover new strengths you never knew you had. ***Yes! Yes! Yes Change!***

19. The Importance of Self-Care

Lesson: You can't pour from an empty cup. Taking care of your mental, physical, and emotional well-being is essential to being able to care for others and live a fulfilling life.

Legacy: Self-care is not selfish; it's necessary. Take time for yourself, and you'll be better able to take care of those around you.

20. Courage to Speak Your Truth

Lesson: Honesty, even when difficult, builds trust and authenticity. Speak your truth with love and integrity, even when it's not the easiest path.

Legacy: Speak your truth, even when your voice shakes. Authenticity is the foundation of strong relationships.

21. Making Peace with the Past

Lesson: The past cannot be changed, but it can be healed. Let go of past regrets and find peace in knowing that your journey has shaped who you are today.

Legacy: Don't let your past define you—learn from it, make peace with it, and use it as the fuel to move forward.

22. The Beauty of Simplicity

Lesson: Often, less is more. Simplifying your life can lead to greater happiness and less stress. Focus on what truly matters and let go of the excess.

Legacy: There's beauty in simplicity. Clear your space, clear your mind, and find joy in the essentials.

23. Live with Integrity

Lesson: Living with integrity means doing what's right, even when no one is watching. It builds trust and respect, both for yourself and from others.

Legacy: Integrity is doing the right thing, even when it's not the easy thing. Stay true to your values, and your actions will always speak louder than words.

24. Forgiving Yourself

Lesson: We are often our own harshest critics. Forgiving yourself is just as important as forgiving others. Treat yourself with the same compassion and understanding you'd offer a friend.

Legacy: Be kind to yourself. You are worthy of the same forgiveness you so freely offer to others.

25. The Value of Humor

Lesson: Life can be serious, but humor is a powerful tool to lighten the load. Laughter creates connection, heals wounds, and makes life a bit more bearable during tough times.

Legacy: Don't take life too seriously—find humor in the chaos. A good laugh can change everything.

26. Gratitude for Life's Small Wins

Lesson: We often wait for big accomplishments to celebrate, but it's the small wins that build the foundation for success. Acknowledge and appreciate every step forward.

Legacy: Every small win is a step toward a greater victory. Celebrate the little things—they are what make the journey worthwhile.

27. **The Importance of Personal Boundaries**
    Lesson: Setting boundaries is not about building walls but about protecting your energy and well-being. Respecting your limits is essential to healthy relationships and personal growth.
    Legacy: Don't be afraid to say no. Protect your peace, and honor your needs as much as you honor others.

28. **Living with Purpose**
    Lesson: A life without purpose can feel aimless. Discovering what truly drives you and pursuing it passionately creates fulfillment and direction.
    Legacy: Find your purpose, and let it guide you. A life lived with purpose is a life well-lived.

29. **Appreciating the Journey, Not Just the Destination**
    Lesson: The journey itself is as important as the destination. Life isn't just about reaching a goal, but about enjoying the process, learning, and growing along the way.
    Legacy: Don't focus only on the destination. The journey holds the lessons and beauty that will shape who you become.

30. The Gift of Listening

Lesson: Listening is a gift that so many people need. Sometimes, the most valuable thing you can offer someone is simply your full attention and empathy.

Legacy: Listen with the intent to understand, not to respond. The greatest gift you can give someone is your presence.

May these legacy lessons flutter softly into the places where your soul is still growing. May they land gently, like butterflies on your shoulder, reminding you that transformation is not just a moment—it's a movement. A journey. A gift. A legacy.

And may your silver pieces of change shine brighter with every fluttering step you take. FLY BUTTERFLY FLY!

ABOUT
THE
AUTHORS

IFEDAYO GREENWAY

Ifedayo is a dedicated mother of three adult children, each living purpose-driven lives aligned with their unique God-given callings and destinies. She is also a proud G-Ma, a dynamic speaker, and a master life coach with a passion for helping women transform their lives.

As the CEO of IG & MORE LLC, she is the visionary behind The Change Experience, an annual event designed to empower women to embrace and navigate their personal change journeys. As the founder of the She Unveils movement, Ifedayo supports aspiring authors in unveiling, writing, and publishing their stories.

A ten-time author and five-time Amazon best-selling author, Ifedayo has published several impactful works, including

Empowered to Become More I, Empowered to Become More II, and The Pathway, The Journey, The Change. As a Visionary Author, she has led transformative collaborative projects such as *Removing the Face, Removing the Fear, Removing the Fragments, A Piece of Change, and A Silver Piece of Change.* She has also co-authored *You Need It, I Got It,* and *Prosper* with two other dynamic visionaries. Her literary work has been featured in *The Huffington Post, CBS, FOX, NBC,* and *Shoutout Atlanta,* showcasing her powerful messages in *Removing the Face and Removing the Fear.* Her inspirational writings have reached thousands through other platforms like Thrive Global and Faith Heart Magazine.

Anchored by a covenant with God to impact lives, Ifedayo draws from her own journey to inspire women to discover their authentic voice and walk boldly in transformation. She lives by her transformational mantra: "Yes! Yes! Yes Change"—a bold declaration that change is not just possible but necessary, intentional, and deeply empowering.

Connect with Ifedayo at: www.igandmore.com

GWENDOLYN WINSTON-MARROW

Gwendolyn Winston-Marrow is the innovator and CEO of Gwen's Inspirational Moments, a platform she uses to inspire and encourage others to keep moving forward. She was married to her beloved husband for over 40 years until his recent passing, and she continues to honor his memory through the work she does. She is a devoted mother, grandmother, and a powerful orator and workshop facilitator. For over 25 years, Gwen has led transformative workshops that exhort, encourage, and empower others to become the motivational force behind their own transformation.

She is passionate about restoration and healing, using the transparency of her own life to show that a place of pain can also become a place of power. Gwen has ministered nationally and internationally and works diligently to fulfill her mission of helping others become the best version of themselves so they may thrive in all they are called to do.

She is also an avid baker, well known for her cheesecakes and pound cakes, which inspired her business Gwen's Slice of Heaven. Everything she does, she does in a spirit of excellence.

Gwen attended Virginia State University, Virginia Commonwealth University, and Fredericksburg Bible College. She was employed by the Department of Social Services and is a former Army Reservist.

Connect with Gwendolyn at: gmarrow.gm@gmail.com

JOYCE FREEMAN

Joyce was born and raised in Norfolk, Virginia. She is the proud mother of a beautiful and caring adult daughter. In May 1989, she earned her undergraduate degree in Public Administration from Norfolk State University. After retiring from a 28-year career with the federal government in October 2013, she went on to receive a Master of Arts degree in Human Services Counseling in May 2019.

Joyce returned to the workforce in 2018, where she works with undergraduate students pursuing a Bachelor of Science degree in Human Services, with a certification in alcohol, addiction, and drug abuse. She has a passion for encouraging others and has been mentoring middle school girls since September 2024 through the Envision Lead Grow's Girl Boss program. In this role, Joyce meets with the girls once a month, providing guidance and support, whether academically or personally, and helping them develop life skills. Additionally, she is dedicated to advocating for women aged 60 and older, engaging in conversations about topics that interest them, such as aging, relationships, and health.

In her leisure time, Joyce enjoys going to the beach, traveling, and listening to all types of music. Her purpose is to encourage and inspire women to recognize the gifts and talents that God has designed for them, to remain confident, and to keep the faith so that they can help others

Connect with Joyce at: jfreeman545@gmail.com

SHERYL L. SCOTT

Sheryl L. Scott is a native of Hampton Roads and currently resides in Northern Virginia. She is a proud mother to two adult children, NaTanya and Ashley, and a Nana to her amazing granddaughter, Marley. With over twenty-five years of experience in the healthcare industry, Sheryl is dedicated to helping seniors and those in need.

In addition to her professional work, she has opened her home to foster pregnant teens and young women, guiding them through some of the most challenging moments of their lives. Her mission is to support, encourage, and empower them to overcome their current circumstances and aspire for a brighter future.

Sheryl is a woman of faith who strives to do the right thing, even if it means sacrificing her own desires. She has a diverse range of interests, including the arts, live theatre, and music, but her greatest joy comes from spending time with her daughters and granddaughter

Connect with Sheryl at: sherylscott2017@yahoo.com

DR. PATRICIA J. WILLIAMS

Dr. Patricia J. Williams is a powerhouse of purpose—an international evangelist, dynamic motivational speaker, educator, and certified personal and executive coach. Her journey proves it's never too late to rise. At 52, she earned her Psychology degree from Old Dominion University, followed by two advanced degrees from Regent University, and completed her Doctorate at 65.

With over 15 years in special education, Dr. Williams has empowered educators and parents to transform the lives of students with disabilities. She is the visionary founder of Abundant Living Consulting, where she leads coaching programs, retreats, and workshops designed to shatter limiting beliefs and ignite personal breakthroughs.

A co-author of Don't Curse Your Crisis, Dr. Williams champions the message that adversity can unlock destiny. Her signature call to action? "You're never too old, never too young, never too anything—if you're willing to leave the land of 'Familiar' and start again." Her mission: awaken purpose, one soul at a time.

Connect with Dr. Patricia at: drpatwms@gmail.com

KIM GREEN

Kim is a native New Yorker who grew up in Queens and earned her Bachelor of Arts in Sociology from Wagner College in Staten Island. With over 40 years of experience as a Personal Banker, she has devoted her career to helping individuals reach their financial goals with care and commitment.

Married to her wonderful husband Anthony for over 37 years, Kim is also the proud mother of adult twins, Ashley and Christopher—the joys of her life. Eighteen years ago, she and her family relocated to Virginia, which they now proudly call home.

Outside the office, Kim is passionate about travel, cooking, and classic movies. She also has a deep heart for ministry, serving faithfully at her church. Whether exploring new places or encouraging others through service, Kim strives to live each day with purpose, compassion, and integrity.

Connect with Kim at: greenkim1@aol.com

SYBIL PERRY

Sybil Perry is a native of Atlanta, Georgia, and a proud U.S. Navy veteran who honorably served for 22 years as a Hospital Corpsman. A dedicated wife of 43 years, loving mother, grandmother, and devout follower of Christ, she attributes all her accomplishments to the grace of God.

Sybil holds degrees in nursing and healthcare administration (BA, BSN, MHSA, MSN) and is currently pursuing her Doctor of Nursing Practice (DNP). She serves as a Registered Nurse and Assistant Nurse Manager with the Veterans Health Administration, where she continues her lifelong commitment to service.

Passionate about faith, family, and community, Sybil enjoys quality time with loved ones and actively serves in her local church. This book chapter marks a bold step in her journey—moving from behind the scenes to the forefront, answering God's call without fear. She hopes her story inspires others to listen for God's counsel, which brings love, healing, and transformation to every part of life.

Connect with Sybil at: seperry56@outlook.com

JACKIE TOGUN

Jackie Togun is an author, educator, entrepreneur, and devoted community resource who remains passionate about elevating health, wholeness, and wellness to the forefront of societal awareness. Residing in Concord, North Carolina. Her life is rooted in worship, enriched by special projects, and guided by a continuous pursuit of growth—especially in love.

She is the proud mother of four adult children. As the oldest of ten siblings, she carries a legacy of leadership and care. She is the proud mother of four adult children and freely extends her nurturing nature to her growing family as a grandmother of ten and great-grandmother of seven.

Jackie was licensed to preach the gospel in May 1995 and ordained in March 2004, faithfully serving in ministry for decades. Her academic achievements include a Bachelor of General Studies in Education and Business Management from Virginia Commonwealth University in Richmond, VA, and a Master of Arts in Education from Oral Roberts University in Tulsa, OK.

Jackie continues to live a life poured out as a servant leader teaching, loving, and leading with grace—as she uplifts individuals and communities through every God-given opportunity.

Connect with Jackie at: 8234befcrn@gmail.com